ORANGE

ORANGE

Doug Angel

authorHOUSE®

AuthorHouse™
1663 Liberty Drive
Bloomington, IN 47403
www.authorhouse.com
Phone: 1-800-839-8640

Published by AuthorHouse   01/28/2013

ISBN: 978-1-4817-0314-7 (sc)
ISBN: 978-1-4817-0313-0 (e)

Foreword

Orange is a small, post industrial town in Western Massachusetts and the site of one of the first commercial sport parachuting centers in the early sixties and where I lived and worked as a jumpmaster and instructor.

Many of the stories in the book are about events that took place there and involve skydiving, but that is not what Orange is really about.

It's about adventure and people: heroes, villains, clowns, astronauts, airplane crashes and a president's son.

A wild party leads to big trouble with an airplane crash on a deserted island. On a dark night in the Mediterranean Sea we hit the rear of the aircraft carrier while trying to land and nursed our crippled bomber toward a small airstrip on the coast of France with fuel gauges on empty.

I've been stalked by a jealous husband who was allegedly armed, busted by cops while shooting a nudie movie which featured a pile of fake pot that looked too real, and flown a small plane into a fog bank over New York City (I'm not a pilot) while the pilot dozed until I had to wake him and admit that we were in big trouble and the FAA police were after us. I never said I was perfect.

I've been fortunate to have lived a long and adventurous life; made over five thousand skydives, survived several airplane crashes, and tried my best to increase the profitability of Smirnoff and cigarette companys.

I hope that you find Orange as entertaining to read as I did to live it.

Chapter 1

An hour ago I was in the middle of this intense dream about a house where I lived with a bunch of people, it's the middle of the night, we get raided by the cops, and a bunch of shit transpires. You know how it flows like that in a dream. I couldn't get back to sleep and started replaying the dream.

I realized that most of it was true, but it was a composite of several events, actually you could call them disasters, that happened to me in a little town in Massachusetts called Orange.

In this dream I'm sound asleep/shitfaced, and I kind of hear something from the other room, banging and voices. Someone opens the door and yells, "Where's Angel?" (That's me).

I get up in my Fruit of the Looms and follow this cop dude into the living room, bright lights blasting my eyeballs and all these people are milling around. It seems there was some minor infraction like underage drinking because this young babe with big tits was wailing and whoever she was there with, seems like his name was Vinnie, was telling her to shut the fuck up, and the cops wanted to see my I.D. so I gave them my drivers license and they wouldn't give it back and I started getting pissy with them (part of it's erased here) and suddenly a bunch of us are sitting on the floor in somebody's house across the street talking about the bust and we get hungry and Mr. Sandwich, a.k.a. Greg, started selling everybody stuff to eat.

Those things usually only happen in dreams but this is one of the real parts of the dream. Greg was a college dropout turned parachute bum who worked for me for a summer at a skydiving center in New Jersey along with his twin brother, John, who flew the jump planes.

Greg was also Mr. Sunglasses and Mr. T. Shirt, depending on what phase of retailing he was specializing in at the time, which was dictated by what wholesale goods were available from his nefarious sources. He was a born salesman; fast-talking, smart, funny, and had no enemies. Greg looked and acted like a surfer and probably would have been doing that rather than jumping out of airplanes if he had grown up in California. The last I heard he'd made a couple of million selling penny stocks and had a forty-foot yacht and a cute oriental wife.

Back in the dream we're sitting around on the floor eating stuff and somebody says that the young chick at the center of the bust is the daughter of a town official and the shit's really going to hit the fan and all of a sudden I'm outside and it's raining and I'm telling myself that tomorrow is going to be hell.

Chapter 2

The Quabbin Gateway Motel Massacre

The real life incarnation of my dream was the Quabbin Gateway Motel Massacre, which always reminds me of the Arlo Guthrie ballad, *Alice's Restaurant*. Each happened in a small town in Massachusetts, both involved real but improbable characters in trouble with local authorities, and both had, for the most part, happy endings.

Orange, and its sister town, Athol, sit at the northern end of the Quabbin reservoir, which was the site of a subsequent disaster that I'll get to later. I ended up there in the mid-sixties, working for a company called Parachutes Incorporated, owned by a rich Frenchman named Jacques who recruited a couple of Ivy League college buddies and started the business of offering same day parachute jump training for the masses.

Orange was a perfect location, a decaying, post-industrial burg that once had thriving paper mills and shoe factories that were now closed or hanging by a thread. The main ingredient was the airport, built during the war for some forgotten military purpose and now an albatross around the neck of the town which was stuck in a million year lease to maintain and operate the triangle made up of three 5000 foot runways. In the center of the triangle lay the second ingredient, a natural sand pit, considered a geological oddity for its non-proximity to the ocean.

For all of his faults (and he had a few), Jacques was a smart guy. When people fall out of airplanes and come down in parachutes they hit the ground. If they hit the ground too hard they sue, even in the sixties. You'd have to be an asshole to hurt yourself in the sand.

Anyway, Jacques and his lawyers bent the good Selectmen of Orange, at a disadvantage due to generations of inbreeding, over the proverbial barrel and gave them a proper hosing. His company, Parachutes Incorporated, would provide a manager and operate the airport, relieving the town of the obligation, and be allowed to operate the parachute Center in return. It was a long lease with the minimal financial aspects structured so that the town would never get a dime.

The Massacre (I don't really know why we called it that but that's the name of the story) took place in the dead of winter around 1967. I was managing the airport and parachute Center, between relationships (not getting laid), and living in a large rundown house in Athol, a couple of miles from Orange, with my two black cats, Super cats #1 & #2. I always have cats.

Though the parachute center was technically open for business all winter there were fortunately very few potential customers stupid enough to want to jump out of a plane with no door when it was below zero on the ground. I still had to keep the airport open, answer phones, and gas the five or six planes that might land there in a typical week.

It was a Monday morning when I answered the call that started the whole thing. P.I. had another parachute Center in Lakewood, New Jersey that I helped build in '63 while on leave from the Navy, and where I worked on weekends until I was transferred to Rhode Island for my last year of duty. Ed, one the Lakewood regulars, and his acolytes, the Boy Skydivers, Bobby, Kenny and

Phil, had decided during the previous evening's vodka and Rolling Rock marathon to pay a visit to uncle Doug. That's me, too.

Their plan, if you could consider anything they did a plan, was to pile into Ed's rusty Cadillac that afternoon and drive six hours to bring me some really good vodka. I had to seem enthusiastic, and it would be good to see them and have my supply replenished, but Ed and the Boys partying in Orange was a situation fraught with danger.

In his late twenties then, with prematurely thinning red hair, a mass of freckles, and perpetually bloodshot eyes, Ed was a piece of work. He held some plebeian position at a company in New York that apparently either didn't care or notice that he wasn't there most of the time. He lived to get wasted. He never ate and drank a fifth of Smirnoff a day. All things considered, he was a good guy!

Bobby, Phil and Kenny were Ed's posse. They were about fourteen when we were building the Lakewood Center and naturally thought skydiving was ultra cool. We let them hang around gave them rides in the ten-place Norseman jump planes while we were getting the place ready to open. Within a year, though they were still legally too young, they started jumping and became the notorious Boy Skydivers.

Lee was the manager of Lakewood and the kids were always hiding from him for one transgression or another. Lakewood, like other Centers, had a minimum opening altitude for skydivers, 2500 feet. It's a good rule. If your main parachute malfunctions you need time to get your reserve open and 2500 feet gives you time to do it. Of course everybody breaks rules. You're just that close to getting a four-way hookup in freefall and the old altimeter is crawling into the red. You know, it happens. But the Boys specialized in it.

When you're fifteen you can't die. They would burn it down to 1200 feet and Lee and I would be waiting for them when they touched down. Grounded for a week, plus polishing the boots and cleaning the toilets. With downcast eyes, toes kicking the sand they'd slink off to perform their penance, but they never learned. When they went out the door and the adrenaline started pumping they just couldn't stop themselves. They were grounded half the summer and Ed was usually with them.

I checked weather after I hung up and there was a serious low pressure system cranking up west of the Berkshires, nothing unusual for this part of the state in January. By late morning the temperature was still in the teens and it was flurrying on and off so I started my pre-blizzard routine; gassing the tractor with the plow on it, filling kerosene cans from the underground tank and checking the security of the hangars where we kept the jump planes.

We had three ten place Noordyn Norsemen, former Alaskan bush planes, shoe-horned into the big hangar and a four place Cessna and a couple of private planes in two smaller hangars that were enclosed on three sides.

I caught up on some paper work and as the approaching storm precluded the possibly of any gas customers, I locked up and drove a mile down the road to Mike's place for a sandwich and a couple of beers.

Mike's was owned of course, by Mike, a rough and tough Orange native in his forty's, barrel-chested and strong as a bull. He was always smiling but that didn't mean anything because when he got drunk he was still smiling when he knocked somebody who had looked at him wrong off of his bar stool.

He liked jumpers though. We brought a good crowd in to eat and drink on weekends and the staff hung out there during the week. He gave me half of my drinks for free and knowing that I wasn't into combat, kept the local rowdies off of my ass.

I played a couple of half-hearted games of pool with Mike's brother, Chris, who was built like his sibling but more dangerous because he loved to fight. I'm not a very good pool player so it wasn't hard to let Chris win, and I always did. It was just better that way.

Snowplow drivers started coming in, downing shots and beers and leaving loaded to drive their trucks all night. The buzz was that we were going to get a foot or more and the winds would be howling.

I chugged a double JD and finished my beer.

"Chicken shit," Mike yelled, "have one on me."

I tossed a few bucks on the bar and threw up my hands,

"Sorry, I've got three hills to climb on bald tires. I don't want to sleep here tonight. Your old lady told me you snore."

There were just a few inches on the ground but the wind was really starting to honk. I followed a plow most the way to Athol and pulled into my garage at dark.

I think I rented that house mostly because of the garage. I had to be at the airport everyday and in the winter if you parked on the street it was guaranteed that the plows would turn your car into a block of ice.

The house wasn't bad, big and old with lots of bedrooms, which seemed silly in the winter when I was usually there alone. But in the summer the place was always full. Jumpmasters needed a place to crash, experienced jumper friends from Boston and New

York came up for the weekends, and lots of babes. My house was party central.

Though I paid the rent, which wasn't much, the visitors brought the booze, food, and weed. The girls cleaned up and cooked on weekends so all in all it was a good deal.

I fed Super Cats #1 & #2, got a fire going in the living room and flipped on the tube. Cable was then a fantasy in some geek's wet dream and my reception was about the same as looking out the window at the blizzard.

The news was all weather. The roads from Boston and New York were all fucked up and the cops were warning everybody to stay home. I thought about Ed and the Boys and considered digging out some bedding and turning on the heat in the spare bedrooms but decided the hell with it. If they made it, which was looking unlikely, I'd take care of it when they got here. If not, I saved the trouble.

But I was sure they were on the way. They didn't have the foresight to avoid driving into a snowstorm and none of them read the papers or watched the news. Once they had a plan they were like a guided missile, a malfunctioning guided missile.

By ten o'clock I had polished off most of a pint of JD, smoked two joints and finished off a leftover Cornish hen and a bag of Oreos. I left the porch light on and the door unlocked (I never locked it anyway), and hit the sack. I was glad the wagon train didn't make it.

Though the plan was to get an early start that day in order to get to Uncle Doug's in Athol before dark, fate intervened. Ed's liquor store was closed and he was forced to detour to a backup source in Queens, which was in the opposite direction of Lakewood where he would eventually pick up the rest of the team. It was after dark as he pulled up to Bobby's middle class house and leaned on the horn. He was persona non grata in the Bobby household due to a previous faux pas, something like pissing in their bathtub.

It's still not clear what temporary insanity caused the Bobby parents to allow their fifteen year old son to accompany a probable felon on a three hundred mile drive in a snowstorm to Uncle Doug's. I guess they thought I was okay.

Kenny was at Bobby's and they jumped in the Caddy and picked up Phil on the other side of town. Phil wasn't a problem; he more or less did what he wanted. But Phil had a girl friend, recently acquired for testosterone related purposes, who turned out to be a whiny bitch. She climbed into the back seat of the Caddy complaining that it was too hot in the car and didn't stop for the next two days. I think her name was Cindy but after the Massacre she was eternally referred to as "I'm too hot, I'm too cold". She did have a great body though.

The storm was approaching from the northwest and though kicking ass in Massachusetts had barely covered the roads to the south as Ed piloted the Cadillac up the Garden State Parkway to the GW Bridge. They opened a couple of Rolling Rocks on the Cross Bronx Expressway and fed Cindy a sleeping pill in a futile attempt to shut her up. The Beatles were blasting out of Ed's state of the art speaker system when they crossed into Connecticut and encountered the first of many obstacles, an overturned tractor-trailer, and big cops with flashlights all over the place.

They rolled all the windows down to de-smoke the car and hot Cindy became "I'm too cold" Cindy. Phil used all of his fifteen-year-old wiles on her; sweet-talk, blowing in her ear, feeling her up. No dice. She bitched for the next hour, in which they covered twenty miles, and finally took another sleeping pill during a piss stop and fell asleep with her head in Phil's lap.

Ed, in deference to the dangerous conditions, Ed cracked open a fifth of Johnny Walker that he thought would improve the chances of his cargo and himself arriving at their destination alive.

The Boys were into vodka with beer chasers and Cindy was snoring.

There is a divine force in the universe that looks out for drunks and children and it bore the travelers to the Massachusetts state line around ten thirty as I was tripping off under my down quilt with Supers #1 & #2 snuggled around my head.

The normally four-hour drive to Orange took seven hours in the now howling blizzard. Kenny sat in the front and wiped the condensation from the windshield with the still comatose Cindy's scarf while Ed artfully steered the Caddy through the drifting snow, lost in an alcoholic haze and grooving to Sgt. Pepper. Bobby and Phil briefly considered a necrophilia game with Cindy but were eventually deterred by some shred of Christian morality that their mentor had failed to wring from them. So they kept drinking.

They plowed into Orange at two in the morning and through the driving snow a miracle appeared in the form of the Quabbin

Gateway Motel, its lonely red vacancy light a beacon in the wilderness. Athol and Uncle Doug's free house were only a few miles away but Ed decided they were pushing their luck and they wheeled up to the office.

Ed had money (he always did), and the Boys never did, but he still didn't like to waste it. They found twenty-seven bucks in Cindy's purse and left her twelve, which everybody agreed was more than fair. Ed went in and rented the room for him and his supposed nephew while Bobby and Phil hid behind the front seat with Cindy's body.

The Polack couple that owned the place made their first mistake by letting red-eyed Ed have room #13 at the farthest end of the motel from the office. He said it was his lucky number. Actually their first mistake was renting him the room in the first place.

Stealthily, they thought, and maybe they kind of were at this point, Ed and the Boys sneaked into the sparse room with their valuables; most of a case of beer, a bottle and a half of Absolute and Cindy, who was slowly whining out of her coma.

I had spent a few nights at the Quabbin Gateway when I was in the Navy at Quonset Point and working as a jumpmaster at Orange on weekends. It was a Motel 6 kind of place, nothing fancy but okay. All of the rooms were the same; two single beds and a fold up in the closet, duck pictures on the wall and two lights, one of which was usually burned out. Oh yeah, and a TV.

There wasn't a phone, so they couldn't call me, and I was sleeping so I wouldn't have answered anyway. They were left to their own devices, and you can imagine what that meant.

Because they were afraid they'd get tired after the long journey they started with ups, even Cindy, which in retrospect was a mistake, progressed to beer and shots, etcetera, etcetera.

At one point they almost talked Cindy into a game of strip poker but she went into the bathroom and started retching loudly and spoiled the mood. Plus she had started her "too hot, too cold" mantra and wanted Ed to take her home. Right!

Never passing up a chance to indoctrinate his followers, Ed started telling stories of past exploits, true and blatantly untrue, but genuinely entertaining and inflammatory.

An example. Ed recalled the time that he threw an M-80 smoke grenade into the toll basket at the Tom's River exit on the Garden State Parkway. Phil staggered out into the blizzard, and it now truly was, and rooted around in the trunk of the Cadillac in an unsuccessful quest for explosives.

Ed was not a fighter, but after he recounted a skirmish with a gay guy in the bathroom at the Red Lion Inn, tall and skinny Bobby punched a hole in the wall between rooms, breaking a finger and exposing the 2 x 4's that supported the Gateway. Phil, who eventually became a college professor, cheerfully relieved the injured Bobby and expanded the hole until there was an unobstructed view into the next room, where they had hoped to view an orgy or at least a couple making out.

Actually they would have been happy if someone was taking a shit but the room was empty as was the rest of the Quabbin Gateway, and it was three o'clock in the morning.

Ed got into an EMT mode and kept opening the door to get snow in the ice bucket for Bobby's broken finger. Cindy was too cold when the door opened, too hot when it was closed, and unlike the story of the porridge, it was never just right. They kept telling her gently to "shut the fuck up."

It took another half hour to finish off the room. Cindy flushed a Kotex with the expected results. Phil and Kenny broke a bed during a wrestling match (Phil won), and Ed threw the lamp that didn't work against the wall in hopes of fixing it. Cindy was continuing to flush the overflowing toilet adding to the incoming tide in the bedroom.

About this time Ed got paranoid, not an unusual state of mind for him. They tried to calm him down but he decided that they had to get out of there, blizzard or no blizzard, and everybody knew better than to argue with him.

They rounded up all the unused alcohol and piled into the Caddy, abandoning the shambles of room 13, definitely unlucky for the motel owners in this case.

They were almost out of the parking lot when Phil made Ed plow back to the room, saying that he'd forgotten something. He staggered inside and re-appeared with the 85 pound Zenith in his arms. Ed popped the trunk, wondering why he hadn't thought of that, and they were on their way.

I wanted to get to the airport early so I had set the alarm for six and was stumbling around with a hangover and my first cup of coffee when Ziggy started banging on the door. I knew it was Ziggy because my front door was one of those old style, fancy glass types with sheer curtains and you could see who was there from almost anywhere in the house, and vice-versa. I didn't care because I usually didn't like to screw in the living room. Ziggy was one of the two town cops.

"Angel," he hissed as I opened the door. We knew each other, of course. Athol was a real small place and in the normal course of human events everybody knows who almost everybody else is. Ziggy and the other town cop hung around the airport from time to time, futilely trying to swoop on the jumper babes or cage free coffee from Neva's restaurant when it was open in the summer season. He was an unpleasant person, even for a cop, skinny and weasely looking with a greasy complexion and piggy eyes. His uniform was always wrinkled. Bits of food usually dotted his tie and shirt and he would come into Mike's with his off-duty .38 bulging in an ankle holster under baggy Levis that hung loosely on his skinny ass. Mike and the regulars tolerated him for obvious reasons but he didn't have a friend in the world.

He came in and brushed the snow off his blue parka.

"You know a guy named Juan Valdez?" he asked as I stared at him through bloodshot eyes, suddenly wondering what leftover evidence was lying around from the night before.

"Ain't he the coffee guy?"

He wiped a dollop of snot onto the back of his leather glove.

"Some guy and his nephew trashed a room at the Quabbin last night. Signed in as Juan Valdez. Stole the television too."

My pulse quickened.

"Never heard of him."

"They was drivin' a Cadillac, black, I think. Polanski said it had a skydive bumper sticker."

Those dumb bastards. I couldn't believe they'd made it. And the worst part was that they were probably still here. Bad shit! I told Ziggy that there weren't any jumpers in the area at this time of year and it was probably some first jump student from Hartford or Boston. Luckily he left before I ran out of bullshit.

I got dressed and warmed up the Rambler, hoping that the fugitives were across the state line by now. The snow had tapered off to flurries but the wind was ripping and there was almost two feet of snow on the ground. The drunken plow drivers had cleared the main road to the airport but they hadn't plowed the driveway so I left the car on the road and walked through knee-deep drifts to the office. As usual the locks were frozen solid and I had to drag a kerosene heater out of the hangar, get it lit in the thirty mile an hour wind, and duct tape the exhaust tube to the lock to start the thawing process.

While I was waiting for results I started the tractor and let it warm up. My hands and face were frozen by now and I headed for one of the small hangars to get out of the wind. As I walked around the corner of the building a large black object, partially covered by a four-foot drift, jutted from the open door. My heart stopped.

I rubbed a peephole in the frost on the driver's side and pressed my face against the window, coming eyeball to eyeball with Ed, holding a bottle of Rolling Rock, surrounded by a cluster of inert forms. He grinned.

"Angel, we made it."

We roused the others and gained access to the warmth of the now unfrozen office where they took turns pissing and throwing up in the bathrooms. Ed wasn't sure how they had made it to the airport but it had apparently been a bitch. Once there they tried to asphyxiate themselves by keeping the car running for heat but luckily ran out of gas before the carbon monoxide took hold. The

Zenith was in a snowdrift on the side of Route 4 due to another Ed paranoia episode.

The phone rang and of course it was Ziggy. He told me that they had found the TV and that the car they were looking for was an old black Cadillac with New York license plates. I told him I was glad about the Zenith and I'd keep my eyes open and hung up. Fuck!

I made a pot of coffee and laid out my stash of Twinkies as we evaluated our options. Cindy was whining that she had to call her mother and Phil told her to shut the fuck up.

Managing the parachute Center had helped me develop a number of skills, not the least of which was crisis management which was what we desperately need now. So I took charge.

Number one, as I saw it, we had to develop some plausible lies. Half of the cops in Massachusetts and Connecticut were looking for them so the chances of running were nil. Number two, Ed's car was full of evidence. We had some detailing to do. Numbers three, four and so on concerned underage drinkers, Bobby and Kenny's parents (Phil's wouldn't give a shit), and whether it would be easier to off Cindy and bury her in the sand pit between the runways rather than trying to get her to keep her mouth shut.

I asked Ed how much money he had, not bothering to ask the Boys having known them since they were fourteen and never seeing more than singles come out of their pockets. To their credit, any money that came their way was spent on skydives which was the way it should be. I didn't bother asking Cindy either, though she and I weren't aware of the robbery and she still thought she had twenty-seven dollars.

Ed assured me that he had his checkbook and could handle the damages at the Quabbin so we went to work. I gave Bobby and Kenny a Shop-Vac and extension cord and assigned them to the Cadillac, called Ziggy and told him I might have some information, was following up on it, and would get back to him in a couple of hours. I didn't want him showing up at the airport unexpectedly.

The real problem was the hotel room, which was badly trashed. If we could pacify Polansky and keep him from pressing charges they might avoid the pokey.

I called Mike. Polansky was a regular at his place and Mike's brother, Chris, was a contractor who could fix anything, drunk or sober, usually the former. Ed and I checked on the car cleaning operation, told the kids where to hide the leftover empty bottles (in the battery compartment of an abandoned van), and waded out to my Rambler. We picked Mike up and briefed him on the way to the Quabbin Gateway. He was still wiping tears from his face when we walked into the office.

I let Ed do the talking and he was eloquent, fortified by something that he had ingested before we left the airport. He was up here on a skiing trip with his absent nephew, he told the owner, and they had a few beers and were horsing around and there was something with the toilet and he tried to fix it, blah blah blah.

Then Mike cut to the chase. How much did he want to get the cops off of their ass? A deal was made. Chris would fix the room, he'd already gotten the TV back, and Ed would give him a hundred bucks for his trouble. We assured him nothing like this would ever happen again and he called Ziggy, who still made us come downtown and get grilled but he was intimidated by Mike's presence and the motel owner wouldn't file charges so he really couldn't do anything anyway. I drove Mike back to his place and we had a couple of shots before I went back to the airport where Cindy and the Boys were drinking Heineken and building a snowman, obviously stoned.

They briefly considered hanging around for the night but I convinced them that no good could come of it so we put a few gallons of aviation fuel in the Caddy and plowed it out. I breathed a sigh of relief as they left the driveway, turned onto Route 4, and headed south.

Though Jacques was in Europe with his Oriental girlfriend it only took him two days to find out. He probably ran up a hundred dollar phone bill chewing me out, even though I didn't do anything, that he knew of anyway, and he banned all the principal players except me from P.I. Centers for life, but that didn't mean shit because he was never around and would forget the whole thing next week.

Oh yeah, Ed's check bounced.

Chapter 3

Now that we've been together for a while, well, a few minutes depending on how fast you read, I guess I should introduce myself. Doug Angel is my real name though virtually every first jump student and reporter for the last forty years has given me the ha-ha, Angel the skydiver routine. It's my name. I can't help it.

I've been working in the sport parachuting business and jumping for forty years so you can pretty well figure how old I am. I didn't start when I was five.

I'm not going to bore you with a lot of statistics but I've made about five thousand skydives and have about two days (48 hours) of freefall time. Are you impressed? I don't care; I just want to justify my qualifications to tell you about the events that are to follow.

Before skydiving took over my life I spent six years in the Navy, flying off carriers as a crewman on a nuclear bomber. Great times, but once I started jumping I couldn't stand the six month Med cruises and got out of the Navy to work for P.I. I stayed there, working at the Centers in Lakewood and Orange until the early 70's when I went to work for a nudie movie company in New York, but that's another book.

I'm a pretty average guy, better than average skydiving instructor, and in all modesty, fairly level headed and not prone to become involved in events that have the potential to lead to trouble, though things didn't always work out that way, as you'll find out in the "Wings Over Water" and "I'm Not Jake" chapters.

I learned most of what I know about running parachute Centers and a lot of what I know about life from my hero and mentor, Nate.

Nate managed the Center at Orange. He was recently separated from his wife, with whom he had spawned four kids

Nate was about 5'8", with a wrestler's stocky build, and strong as a bull. He was a born pilot, trained by his father, Batch, from the time he could see over the windscreen and reach the rudder pedals, and could fly anything with wings. He particularly enjoyed the Norsemen, the giant, ungainly bush planes that were more like driving a truck than flying. P.I. owned about ten of them at one point. They were constructed of wood and fabric, powered by a large radial engine and all over forty years old. They were Nate's pride and joy. In addition to flying jumpers he did virtually all of the maintenance on the fleet and managed the airport and parachute center in the summer and worked on ski patrol in the winter.

After getting a degree at an Ivy League college he joined up with Jacques and helped build Orange and get it up and running. In 1962 the World Parachuting Championships were held there and in addition to being host he competed for the U.S. team in the style and accuracy competition.

Nate and I shared a house in Athol for a couple of years while I was in training to be a P.I. manager and it became nationally known as the parachuting place to party on the east coast. It was on the same street and of the same style as the one I lived in when the Quabbin Gateway Massacre took place several years later. An old two story frame with lots of bedrooms and not much furniture but the price was right and it was far enough from the nearest neighbors to keep them from calling the cops if things got too rowdy, which was every weekend.

Nate and I both liked to cook, made our own beer, and didn't have to pay for jumps, so we lived quite well considering the meager wages we received.

Our days off were Tuesdays and Wednesdays and about every other week Nate would fly down to Lakewood on Monday night after we closed the Center, to visit Jill, a charming British girl who ran the office and the jumper manifest at Lakewood. I would sometimes accompany him on these trips and crash and party with the Lakewood jumpmasters who had a couple of communal houses.

One Monday we closed early and threw our overnight bags in the back seat of 88 Charlie, our Cessna 180, a four-place tail dragger jump plane. All of the seats, except the pilot's, and the door on the right side, had been removed for jumping so Nate put the right front seat back in and re-installed the door while I gassed up. The flight took about two hours so I filled the tanks only half way, enough to get there with a little reserve because we were paying for the gas ourselves and we could buy it for a dime a gallon cheaper at Lakewood due to state tax or some shit. I never liked this idea because one thing you obviously never want to do in an airplane is run out of gas. But I never argued with Nate about airplanes. It would be like arguing with Lindbergh.

I have good reason to be nervous about these matters. When I was flying off of carriers we would often return from a four-hour mission, at night, in bad weather, with twenty or thirty minutes of fuel left and have to compete with fifteen or twenty planes in the same situation to catch a wire or splash in the middle of the Atlantic. It happened a lot.

We took off just after sunset and pointed 88 Charlie south. Nate was teaching me to fly and though I wasn't ready to take off or land the 180 yet, I knew enough about airplanes to fly it pretty well once we were in the air. There are two yokes so if I did anything really stupid Nate could always save our lives.

We climbed out over the Quabbin reservoir, leveled off at three thousand feet and set the trim. In twenty minutes we were through the Hartford control area and Nate turned the controls over to me and got ready to take a nap.

This isn't as stupid as it sounds. For the next hour, until we got close to Lakewood, we would be over rural Connecticut and Long Island then down the Jersey coast and I'd made the trip enough to not get lost. Plus, Nate really needed to take a nap. I don't know where he'd spent the previous night or with whom but he dragged his ass home that morning, red-eyed and disheveled, just in time to take a shower and get to the airport and fly all day. He gave me headings and was snoring in five minutes.

The night was clear and black with no sign of a moon. I adjusted the trim a bit, and checked my altitude and heading by the dim, red, instrument lights. A-O-K.

As I droned along the red panel lights made me think of my Navy days, a few years before.

I wasn't a pilot. In fact after I joined the Navy I was trained as an aviation electrician and sent to a Heavy Attack squadron based in Sanford, Florida. There were six or seven of the same squadrons at the base, all flying A3D Skywarriors; twin jet bombers that were the largest planes that flew off carriers. Our mission was to deliver conventional and nuclear bombs.

The squadrons at Sanford, including ours, would deploy once a year to an aircraft carrier and cruise the Mediterranean Sea as a deterrent to the bad guys during the cold war. The Russians were the bad guys then.

The other six months we were mostly at Sanford with a few short trips to Guantanamo Bay, Cuba (we all know where that is now) so the crews could practice carrier landings to stay qualified. After I was in the squadron for a few months I found out that there were openings for flight crewmembers and applied. I really wasn't cut out for the electrician gig and flight crew pay would add an extra ninety dollars to my measly two hundred a month.

I was accepted and spent about three months in crew school and two weeks in a nuclear weapons course. I was issued a bright orange flight suit, survival vest, a .38 revolver, and took to the sky.

There were three of us in the crew; pilot, bombardier/navigator, and third crewman (me). My job was to operate the twin 20mm tail guns and perform celestial navigation. I was also responsible for pre-flight and packing the drogue 'chute that helped us slow down on land.

Though I had many experiences in my Navy flying days the one that I was recalling on the flight to Lakewood was not about carrying bombs but booze.

When we weren't on the ship, one of our planes would make a booze run about once a month from Sanford to Guantanamo where you could buy a forty ounce bottle of the best scotch for a couple of bucks. The pilots and crewmen would make a list of what they wanted, pony up the money, and one of our crews would fly down to Cuba, do the deal, and come back with the goods. But it wasn't quite that simple.

Even though we were the Navy it was illegal due to customs, and if we got caught a thousand bucks worth of hooch would be down the drain and everybody's money lost.

There were two customs officials permanently stationed at Sanford and they were supposed to check any planes coming from outside the country for illegally smuggled goods. Being government employees they were obviously pricks and not even decent enough to accept bribes. But there was a way around the problem.

Almost every night planes from our squadron would be practicing carrier landings on the runway. They were called FCLPs field carrier landing practice, which entailed circling in the flight pattern and taking turns touching down to simulate catching an arresting wire on a carrier and immediately taking off again to circle back for another pass. The booze flight would make a couple of passes and leave the pattern, fly to Cuba, load up and fly back and join the other practicing planes, land, and taxi into our hangar where the customers would claim their booty.

It was our turn one night in June and we took off with a briefcase stuffed with cash, made a couple of FCLPs and turned out of the pattern and headed south. My pilot, a Lt. Commander named Larry, climbed to thirty thousand feet and we touched down at Guantanamo in less than an hour.

We taxied to the pre-arranged pick-up spot and handed over the cash to a couple of low level PX sailors who helped us strap the cases of liquor onto the catwalks inside the bomb bay and we were airborne again in an hour. Smooth.

Fifteen minutes later we were at thirty thousand feet again and just about to enter controlled airspace around Miami when several things happened at once. A warning light came on in front of Billy, the bombardier, indicating that our pressurization system was failing. At the same time I started to hear small popping explosions from the bomb bay.

Larry pushed the yoke forward and dove the A3D toward breathing altitude, telling me and Billy to go to one hundred percent oxygen. I pressed my intercom button and told him that something was going on in the bomb bay and I was going back to have a look.

He was on the radio with Miami air traffic control alerting them to our problem and asking clearance to pass through their area at a lower altitude as I un-strapped and crawled laboriously through the tunnel to the bomb bay, impeded by my parachute and survival gear.

I swung the hatch open and the popping was louder and interspersed with multiple loud hissing sounds. I panned my flashlight around the bay looking for the source of the trouble and as the beam passed over our cargo I discovered the problem. Champagne!

We had loaded ten cases in Cuba. The corks were exploding from the depressurization, geysers of white foam spurting into the air. I was glad that it all belonged to the officers. I drank JD.

I crawled back to the cockpit to report my findings. We had leveled off at 15,000 feet and Larry was arguing with the air traffic guys. He got off the radio and when I told him what was going on in the back he just laughed. That was a minor problem, as it turned out. Miami wouldn't let us enter their control area below 25,000 feet. We couldn't climb back up without pressurization. Catch 22.

We'd have to declare an emergency and land at Miami. And go through customs!

We only had one option. Larry called Miami back and told them we were declaring an emergency and got permission to descend to five thousand and orbit over the water to burn off fuel. I crawled back to the bomb bay and plugged into the intercom station so I could talk to Larry and Billy. Squatting on the catwalk next to the cargo I secured myself to the bulkhead with a cargo strap, pulled my survival knife out of the sheath on my leg and pressed the intercom button.

"I'm ready," I told them.

Larry had slowed the plane to a hundred and fifty knots and Billy opened the bomb doors, exposing the black water a mile below. Every time I watch *Dr. Strangelove* I get flashbacks. And I hadn't even made my first jump yet.

I cut one of the ropes and starting rolling the cases into freefall: Moet Chandon, Johnny Walker Red, Jack Daniels (that one hurt). Thirty-seven cases, bombs away. Fishermen beware.

Billy closed the doors and I got back to the cockpit and strapped myself in for landing. Fuck customs.

Back in the Cessna, I thought, "this is fun." The engine drowned out Nate's snoring and I browsed over the panel; oil pressure and temp, rpm's at 2400, manifold pressure in the green. You didn't have to worry about an engine failure on a plane that Nate maintained.

I reached the southern coast of Connecticut and figured I was a little too far west which would bring me into the New York control area and require working with controllers in the restricted airspace which Nate always avoided, and I didn't know how to do that anyway, so I kicked in a ten degree left correction with the rudder and started across Long Island Sound.

Though there weren't any clouds, the visibility had decreased a bit which I figured was industrial haze from the city. I dropped down to twenty five hundred feet and it seemed better as I passed five miles east of Kennedy Airport and headed across Raritan Bay toward the Sandy Hook lighthouse.

There were some patches of ground fog in the bay and the visibility was getting troublesome again so I dropped another five hundred feet and thought about waking Nate. Nah! I'd be past Sandy Hook in a couple of minutes and from there it was just follow the Jersey shoreline to Lakewood, another twenty minutes away. I had it under control and wanted to wait until we were in the pattern to put the real pilot on duty.

I think it was around Red Bank when the shit hit the fan. Clouds? Fog? I don't know. All of a sudden I couldn't see the ground. I started sweating and eased the nose over and at twelve hundred feet I came out of it and breathed a sigh of relief. A little low but I knew it was all flat terrain between here and our destination so I didn't wake Nate until I flew into a white-out five minutes later.

He looked out the window and grabbed the controls.

"Angel, where in the fuck are we?" he yelled at me.

I gave him a very accurate fix and started to make excuses but he put me to work dialing radio frequencies and pulling out sectional charts.

"We're fucked," he said, to cheer me up. Sorry Nate.

Based on my information that the visibility had been okay when I passed New York, Nate went down to five hundred feet and did a one eighty, heading north, back up the coast. Pursuing us from behind was a fog bank rolling in from the ocean, unusual but not unheard of. When they happened the visibility could drop from clear to zero in minutes. And it was happening.

Nate decided to maintain radio silence. I knew we hadn't filed a flight plan and the plane wasn't rated to fly in instrument conditions, which we were definitely in. There were going to be lots of papers to fill out and FAA guys to talk to if we got caught flying around in New York airspace at five hundred feet.

We tuned the VOR navigation radio to Teterboro Airport, just across the Hudson River from Manhattan, and stayed far enough south to avoid hitting a skyscraper. Aircraft controllers were aware that some assholes were crop dusting through the restricted airspace but we weren't talking and were too low for them to follow us on radar. I checked the fuel gauges and figured that we had about fifteen minutes left before it wouldn't matter if we found Teterboro or not.

Sweat poured down Nate's clenched jaw (he always clenched his jaw when something serious was going on.) He stared intently through the cockpit window. We were at 300 feet and in and out of fog when we spotted the rotating beacon on the Teterboro tower. Nate banked hard and slipped the Cessna sideways, plunking it down on the end of the seven thousand foot runway.

We took the first turn-off, still almost a mile from the tower, and ignored their radio calls for the aircraft landing at Teterboro to identify itself. There were hundreds of small planes tied down at the airport and that saved our ass. We taxied with our lights out until we found an empty tie-down and were home free. Sneaking into the terminal, we tried to maintain a low profile, called Jill collect and told her that we needed to be rescued. She was there in an hour and we were back in Lakewood an hour later celebrating our near demise.

There was some small hassle about a landing fee when we retrieved the plane on Thursday morning but they never pinned anything on us. Nate eventually forgave me but never stopped breaking my balls about the episode and I never did learn to fly.

Chapter 4

MSB

For the last forty years, on the twenty-first of June, I have attended or hosted a Mid-Summer Night's ball. I think Nate started them when he was in college and he taught me the routine. I upheld the tradition after he got out of the business

The MSB is held to celebrate the longest day of the year, the Summer Solstice, with a no-holds barred party. It includes drinking, debauchery, and roasting a pig, which takes about eight hours, allowing adequate time to warm up for the main event.

At Orange and Lakewood we usually held the event in the sand bowls where the jumpers land, the idea being that there would be fewer casualties. There were many MSBs and every one was a story by itself but one of the most memorable took place in Lakewood in the mid-sixties. It also featured Jake.

Jake was a friend of Nate's from Aspen, a ski bum turned jump bum in the summer. Nate, by the way, was also an expert skier and went out west every winter to teach skiing and work on the ski patrol in Aspen or Vail. He usually brought back a couple of friends and hired them to work at various jobs at one of the parachute Centers in the summer. Hence Jake.

Lean and wiry with long, rough-cut blond hair, Jake was a piece of work. Probably in his early twenties then, missing a front tooth and with a gravely whisky voice, he would have been the perfect snowboard dude if they had been invented then. He was funny and fearless and the most successful pussy magnet I ever met. He would walk into a bar, chat up a beautiful chick he'd never met, who was there with her husband or boyfriend, screw her in the bathroom or parking lot, and she'd buy him a drink before they parted. I never figured out how he did it.

So the MSB was approaching. We had deviated from the sand bowl plan that year and had decided for reasons of privacy or whatever to hold it at the dry lakes, an area in the pinewoods adjacent to the airport that consisted of two shallow ponds surrounded by sand pits, and more important, in the middle of nowhere.

Some of the disadvantages were no access to electricity or sanitary facilities, which was not a problem for the guys, who are used to, and probably prefer, pissing in the woods. But the girls bitched and because it was the '60's we didn't pay any attention. Oh, and the pinewoods were full of very large, black, hideous pine snakes. They were all over the place, hanging in the trees and everywhere in the underbrush. I've seen them up to seven feet long and as big around as a man's bicep. Harmless, but everybody hated them. Guess that's why the girls didn't want to squat in the bushes.

A few days before the event we ordered a pig from a local farmer, a forty pounder as I recall, guaranteed to be fresh killed and delivered to the airport early morning on the day of the Ball. The twenty-first that year fell on a Tuesday which was good luck because the Center wasn't open on Tuesday and Wednesday and we had the whole day and night to party and the next day to recover.

Jake was working at Lakewood then and he and I were crashing at Bill's house on a spit of land that jutted into Barnegat Bay. Bill was a jumpmaster at Lakewood, presently separated from his old lady and getting used to the single life again. He wasn't tall, only about five-four, with a ruddy complexion, and a missing index finger. He said he'd lost it on purpose because he wanted to be like our hero, Nate, also minus a digit.

At this time Jake had a broken leg, either left over from the ski season or acquired at the beginning of the jump season, and had a cast up to his thigh that he was anxious to get removed on the twenty-second, the day after the Ball.

At the crack of nine on the day of the Ball, Jake, Bill, and I whipped over to the airport where the Pig Guy and the Boy Skydivers were waiting for us. We checked out the pig, laying naked and unashamed in a box of ice, and turned over the forty bucks.

The kids got the beat up Ford pick-up we used to haul parachutes from the landing area to the rigging loft, loaded the pig, bags of charcoal, and a shovel and we headed for the dry lakes, winding through the pine woods on rutted fire roads blanketed with brown pine needles.

Because there had been a rainy spring, the dry lakes were still wet, probably a few feet deep, and looked like two side by side swimming pools, a hundred yards square with sandy beaches surrounding them. The atmosphere was somewhat spoiled by fifty thousand volt, cross-country power lines that towered several hundred feet overhead, but hey, you can't have everything.

We cracked a beer while the kids unloaded the truck and dug a pit for the pig fire. The kids always had to do the shit work but that was fair. First of all they were kids. We provided their beer because they were all under age and never had any money, and most important, they always owed us from their never-ending fuck-ups that required paybacks in the form of slave labor. It was a symbiotic relationship and though they might bitch and moan they followed orders.

When the charcoal was fired up we sodomized the pig with a sturdy spit of green wood, to the great amusement of the Boys, and hung it a couple of feet above the fire. We left them with a six pack and final instructions to oversee the roasting.

We dropped the truck off at the airport and piled into my beat up, shitty-brown Rambler and headed for the Bricktown shopping center to buy the food and stuff for the party, detouring into the restaurant conveniently located next to Shoprite, with the not very original name of Mom's.

We were red-eyed and ravenously hungry, laughing at stupid things and generally making a spectacle of ourselves but the regulars had seen it before and didn't pay much attention. Jake made a halfhearted move on a homely waitress and Bill remembered that he'd left his beer can dog in the Rambler and brought it in and tied the leash to our table leg. The day was getting off to a fine start.

It took an hour or so to finish the shopping and we headed back to the airport, stopping at the dry lakes to check on the pig team, who were dozing in the sun, surrounded by empty beer cans. The fire was almost out and the pig was starting to look like something out of *The Lord of the Flies*. We douched it off with a gallon of water from the shopping trip and chewed the kids out, giving them a lecture on responsibility and the importance of their mission, not that it would make any difference but as their leaders we felt it was our duty.

We spent the rest of the afternoon getting stuff ready for the Ball, taking frequent beer breaks and checking on the pig operation.

At five o'clock sharp the Norseman from Orange, with Nate at the controls, appeared from behind the pine trees and made a high speed buzz job no more than a hundred feet above the ground.

When they landed and shut down it looked like one of the clown cars in the circus. Fifteen people piled out of the ten-place aircraft, all looking for someplace to take a piss. About half of the passengers were local girls from Orange, a couple obviously underage and brought across state lines for indecent purposes, I was thinking the indictment would read.

We unloaded the home brew, tied the plane down and started ferrying people and supplies to the party site in the pick-up. Nate and Jake took charge of cooking while the rest of us broke into the beer and started trying to establish meaningful, loving, relationships for the evening.

Thunderheads had been building throughout the afternoon and occasional flashes of lightning could be seen in the distance to the southwest. If you wanted to pick a day of the year that you could be guaranteed to see a thunderstorm, June twenty-first would be your best bet. I think at least half of the MSBs have been punctuated by torrential downpours and lightning bolts slamming into the ground in close proximity to the sinners in attendance, not that it affected the event in any serious way, and certainly not stopping it.

Around sunset Nate and Jake declared the pig cooked and we dug the side dishes out of coolers and chowed down. Remembering the gathering of flies that morning and the inherent danger of trichinosis, I opted for burgers.

After we dined, sitting in the sand with our paper plates balanced on our laps, we built a bonfire in the pig pit and started bolstering the home brew with shots of JD and moonshine, courtesy of Ed, toasting companions who had moved on to the big drop zone in the sky through some act of God or ill advised adventure. We smoked some more, went skinny-dipping in the dry lakes, and some of the weaker stomachs retreated to the pine woods from time to time, snakes or no snakes.

It was probably midnight when Jake decided to do his tree trick. Jake loved to climb trees and he was really good at it. He would literally leap around in the top of a tree like an ape, swinging from limb to limb. Whenever a student jumper would land off the drop zone and be hanging fifty feet up in a pine tree Jake would come to the rescue. He loved it.

I tried to remind him that he still had a cast on but he had that look in his eye so I backed off and shined the spotlight from the pick-up on the hundred foot oak that grew among the pines and Jake started up, to the cheers of the crowd and the accompaniment of lightening bolts and a rising wind.

The cast was more of an encumbrance than he had reckoned on in his impaired state and though it took him twenty minutes he climbed as high as the branches would support him.

Now usually at this point (I had seen him perform his routine on numerous occasions, drunk and sober, it made no difference to Jake) he would swing from branch to branch but the cast was impeding him and he was running out of steam so he went right into the finale which entailed dropping through the branches in an almost free fall mode, catching a limb briefly on the way down to slow himself enough to keep from splattering on the ground.

I followed him with the spotlight as he started the plunge; girls screamed, lightning flashed, and down came Jake, an almost perfect execution. Almost perfect because he missed the last branch and fell about fifteen feet with nothing to slow him down.

He hit the sand, which probably saved his life, as sheets of rain pelted the spectators and the storm crashed around us. We ran over to him as he tried to get up, spitting sand. He grinned and looked proud.

"How'd I do?" he asked, as we helped him to his feet and he hobbled off to get a shot and beer.

The rain was pounding the shit out of us and Jake wasn't feeling too good so we gave up around one o'clock and Bill, Jake, and I went back to Bill's house and I smoked a joint, gave Jake a sleeping pill and put him to bed.

Bill and I sat in his kitchen for a while, reviewing the evening's events. We had a severe hunger attack and found a bowl of week-old spaghetti in the fridge that was approximately the consistency of hard plastic, which we split and fought over the shreds in the bowl.

Bill had to meet with a divorce lawyer in the morning so I set my alarm for eight so I could drive Jake to the doctor where he was due to have his cast taken off. As usual, Jake was on the revoked list.

I rapped on his bedroom door, heard him moaning (from his hangover I thought) and went in. He was sitting naked on the side of the bed.

"My fucking leg," he groaned.

I told him to get dressed and we'd go get the cast off and he'd feel better. He shook his head.

"Not that one, the other one."

The doctor took the cast off of the leg that was now healed and put one on the other that was broken in two places.

Chapter 5

Nectar of the Gods

We had this really ancient twenty gallon ceramic crock that Nate had bought at some flea market. The crock was so heavy that it took two people to lift it when it was empty, and full, no way. It was perched on concrete blocks in the bathroom in our house in Athol, in a place of honor next to the toilet. We had it on blocks to make it high enough so no one could accidentally or maliciously piss in it. We would have guests from time to time who couldn't always be trusted.

When our bottled beer was down to a three-week supply it would be time to start a new batch. Timing would be critical. If we ran out we'd be forced to drink the commercial stuff and worse, have to pay for it.

The first step would be to buy the ingredients which meant a trip to Greenfield, about forty-five minutes from Orange, the only place that had cans of malt. The place was a run-down hardware/ grocery store with cluttered shelves and some old fart half-asleep behind the counter. As soon as he saw us come in he'd go to a dungeon-like back room and return with a dust-covered box with one-quart cans of malt with some Indian name. We'd buy a half dozen cans and a box of bottle caps and head back to the Acme in Athol for the other stuff; ten pounds of sugar and a bunch of yeast cakes.

Back home, Nate would get on his hands and knees in the bathroom and scoop handfuls of the gooey malt from the cans, dissolving it in small quantities of water that moi would fetch from the kitchen as needed. When the malt was pretty well soup he mixed in the proper quantities of yeast until it was all blended together. He never referred to any written instructions. I'm not sure there even were any, but the beer was always great.

The last step was to fill the crock with water, give it a few stirs, cover it with a piece of cheesecloth, and wait for nature to take its course, usually in about two weeks.

In the interim, usually on our Tuesday day off, we'd start rounding up bottles. We always saved them at the house but we took beer to the airport, down to Lakewood, to other parties, so we were always having a problem with bottle slippage

We'd stop by Mike's place but he usually wouldn't give us any because he had to return them to the distributor for the deposit and he didn't like the idea of us competing with him in the first place. Another source was the alley behind the VFW where we would sometimes find a case or two put out with the garbage. If we were lucky we might come up with five cases of empties for a day's work. These were supplemented with a few here and there that friends would save for us but we were always a little insecure in the bottle department.

Once we had enough bottles we'd have a washing operation, building a fire under a washtub of water in the back yard and boiling a case at a time to disinfect them. Because many of our sources were suspect it wasn't unlikely that some of the bottles were used for everything from sex toys to repositories for various body fluids, and we really didn't want to kill anybody.

When the bottles were sanitized they were sorted by size, from Rolling Rock up to quarts, and put in empty cases in the cellar.

The fermentation period, as I told you, was a couple of weeks, but you didn't have to count the days to know when the stuff was about ready. No matter the time of year, one morning as you stood in front of the toilet a squadron of Drasfilio Melanogaster of the fruit fly sub-species would be circling the vat of beer. After we first noticed the flies blessing the batch we knew that in three days it would be ready to bottle. It's just one of those unexplainable miracles.

If bottling day didn't fall on a Tuesday, when we were off, we'd blow off as much business as we could at the Center and leave some junior jumpmaster in charge so we could get the job done. We had our priorities.

Nate and I would line the bottles up by size in the kitchen and try to find the capper, an important cog in the operation. It was usually under a bed or stuck in a remote corner of an unused closet. You can't bottle beer without the capper. And for the capper you have to have shims. The bottles, you may remember, are not all the same size, they are four different sizes and each size requires a shim underneath to bring the top of the bottle into a position for the capper to press the cap on. The shims were brick, board, or shingle depending on the bottle. Of course one size didn't need a shim because the capper was made for that type but almost none of the bottles we ended up with were that kind.

Scooping a few gallons at a time from the vat, Nate would transport it to the kitchen where I would carefully funnel two teaspoons of sugar into each empty bottle. He followed me down the line filling each bottle to the top with ambrosia. When a few dozen bottles were ready we'd shift to capping, Nate yelling, brick, board, shingle as needed from his apprentice, and commenting on the appearance of the batch.

The project took most of the day and when a batch was bottled and safely nestled in cases in the cool, dark, basement for ten days of aging, it was traditional to celebrate, not that we ever needed a reason. And we always had company because somehow people we hardly knew would, like Drasphilio Melanogaster, suddenly appear, dropping in to say hello.

"Hey, makin' a new batch?" they'd ask. Orange is a real small town.

Chapter 6

Night Fall

Days at the parachute center were long and we worked hard but when we were done for the day or the Center was closed on Tuesdays there were two places where we ate and drank in Orange; Mike's Place, of course, and The Inn.

There was a good-sized field adjacent to the Inn, the only clearing for a mile around and surrounded by very tall trees. On Saturday and Sunday nights experienced jumpers and staff would jump into the field on the last flight of the day and compete for a free steak dinner for closest to the target. You could sit at the bar and watch the action through huge glass windows or sit outside and have a joint to enhance your appetite.

Knowing this, you probably won't understand why Kenny, John, Curt and I decided to make a night jump into the Inn, a sixty-second freefall from thirteen thousand feet. I'm sure it started with a few cocktails, tales of previous jumping exploits, probably some chicks there that we wanted to splash our macho-ness on. I don't remember but we thought it would definitely be cool.

We had a good chance of pulling it off without seriously damaging ourselves. John was a jumpmaster at Orange with over a thousand jumps, Kenny had five hundred or so, and Curt, a rich stockbroker up from Lakewood had a couple of thousand, and he'd only been jumping for three years. It helps to have money.

Nate agreed to fly 88 Charlie on the mission. There were only four of us and Nate so there was no need for the noisy, high visibility Norseman to attract attention, for we had no intention of attempting to convince the Massachusetts Aeronautic Commission and the FAA that they should issue us a waiver for a night jump into the Inn.

Pat, a part-time jumpmaster for P.I., and full-time lineman for a Boston electric company, volunteered to be ground crew and gave us a demonstration of a high intensity strobe light, cutting-edge technology at the time, that he was going to use to help us see the field from two miles up.

On the night of the jump we waited until everyone had left the airport and went over our plan. We had the jumpmaster on the last flight of the day throw a wind streamer at the Inn so we could figure how far upwind we should get out of the plane to make it into the landing area.

Nate checked high altitude winds with flight service and they were light, as they usually are in the summer, and wouldn't be a factor. We gave Pat a hand held ground-to-air radio tuned to our business frequency that no one else usually listened to in case he had to call the jump off for some reason, and he headed up to the Inn.

Our main consideration was making sure we all got into the landing area. If you were in the woods or on the other side of the hill in Lake Mohawk, you had a big problem. Anyone that missed had to make it to Mike's place within two hours after which we'd have to come clean and call the cops, search and rescue, and our lawyers.

While Nate warmed up the plane we strapped night flares on our feet and stashed flashlights in our jumpsuit pockets. We were going to try to do a four way hook-up in freefall and the flares would help us see each other. The flashlights would give us enough light to cut our wrists if we landed in the trees.

We climbed aboard and Nate did a final run up and took off to the south, away from town and inquiring minds.

We didn't talk on the way up. It's so noisy in the plane that it's not worth the trouble to try. The only lights inside the Cessna are the red instrument lights at night so you really can't see each other very well either. I was going to spot; look out and pick the place and time to exit the airplane, so I concentrated on my plan and re-ran it in my head to occupy the time it took to climb to jump altitude.

I was sitting on the floor by the jump door next to Nate and he looked at me a couple of times, smiled, and shook his head. I knew he was just trying to fuck with my mind. If he hadn't volunteered to fly us he would have been making the jump.

When we reached jump altitude the other guys got off of the floor and turned around on their knees, preparing for the exit as I hung my head out in the prop blast and gave Nate left and right corrections with my thumb. I waited until we were about five hundred yards upwind of the field, yelled "cut" and climbed out onto the small wooden jump step. The rest of the crew crammed themselves to the edge of the door and poured out as I popped my flare and back-looped off the step.

I stabilized on my back and watched their silhouettes burst into color a hundred feet above me, phosphorous sparks streaming from their ankles as we accelerated to terminal velocity.

As my fellow fliers approached my level I arched my back and flipped over, stomach to earth in the normal free fall position. I looked down to see if I could pick up the strobe but from that

altitude and falling at one hundred and twenty miles per hour
it was just a dark pit with scattered points of light. It didn't
matter anyway now, we were committed, or, I thought, should be
committed.

John was the hottest relative work jumper and he closed in on
me first, a soft glowing ball of light gliding gracefully through the
blackness. He grabbed my wrist and we grinned at each other and
started a slow three sixty, looking around for Curt and Kenny. I
glanced at my wrist altimeter and saw the needle swing past nine.
Another forty seconds of free fall left.

Kenny caught up with us at eight thousand, flaring out of a two
hundred mile an hour head down dive and grabbed each of our
open hands. We rotated left then right looking for Curt's flare but
there was no sign of him so we relaxed and enjoyed the fall.

At thirty five hundred feet we gave a shake to acknowledge
break off altitude and did a one eighty turn and tracked away from
each other for opening. I pulled at twenty-five hundred and felt
the pilot chute and bag lift off of my back. I never worry about my
parachute opening but if I was going to have a malfunction I sure
hoped it wouldn't be now. If I had to cut away my main 'chute and
open a non-steerable reserve there would be a one percent chance
of making the field and a ninety-nine percent chance of being in
the woods. The Para Commander popped open on schedule and I
fished the flashlight out of my pocket and shined it up, checking
the canopy. All systems go.

I tried to get my bearings. It's very disorienting hanging a
half-mile up in the dark. I knew the area so well from the air that I
could stick my head out of the door in the daytime and even if we
were miles from the airport know exactly where I was. This was

some other shit. I finally picked out the ridge of the hill that the Inn was located on and saw a sliver of moonlight glinting off of Lake Mohawk on the other side. I looked almost straight down and lo and behold, the strobe, blink, blink, blinking.

"Hell of a spot Angel," I thought, and looked for my partners. The flares were burnt out by now but I could see occasional points of light from the other guys' flashlights and adjusted my altitude so we wouldn't all be landing at the same time, and possibly collide.

When we were about a minute from landing Pat turned on a portable searchlight so we could see the target, a white X with a six-inch dead center disk at the intersection. I could see Kenny a few hundred feet below me setting up for his final approach and John's flashlight winked a hundred yards to my left at about the same altitude that I was at. I did a couple of 360's to drop a little below him and looked around for Curt who was still missing in action.

Kenny touched down about fifty yards from the target and I started my approach, braking the P.C. by pulling both steering toggles half way down and making small lateral adjustments to stay aligned with the target. I thought I was going to nail the dead center disc but hit a little burble ten seconds from touchdown that put me 15 feet left of the center of the X. John was right on my tail and beat me by a couple of feet.

No sign of Curt. Pat said he thought he saw his flare disappearing over the top of the ridge but wasn't sure. We were inclined to think that he was mistaken because the flares only burned for sixty seconds and would have been out around the time he opened. We gathered up our gear and made a getaway in Pat's car.

We spent a half hour cruising the road to the Inn and the other side of the hill, stopping every hundred yards or so to yell into the woods. The moon was higher now and we scanned the surface of the lake before giving up and drove down to Mike's Place as planned and started drinking, exuberant, but a bit nervous about our missing partner.

Nate showed up a few minutes after we got there and agreed that we should wait for another hour or so before taking any drastic action. The last thing we wanted to do was get the cops involved and have the aviation authorities find out which would guarantee serious trouble including possibly losing our licenses and heavy fines.

At eleven thirty, five minutes before the two-hour deadline to start a search, Curt burst through the door with his parachute under his arm, trailed by the local yokel that had given him a ride. Leaves and sticks were falling out of his gear and he had gashes on his arm and neck, garnished with dried blood.

"Gimme a fucking beer," he yelled at us, and the motley crew of barflies.

As soon as he'd left the plane, he told us, his goggles fogged over and he was totally blind during the freefall. He made several futile attempts to wipe them off and because he couldn't see his altimeter, decided to pull, even though he thought he was still well above opening altitude. Once the 'chute was open he pulled the goggles off and looked at his altimeter which read seven hundred feet as he drifted down the back side of the ridge towards Lake Mohawk.

He unhooked one side of his belly mount reserve and released his chest strap to prepare for a water landing but fell short of the lake and crashed through the trees, ending up hanging about fifteen feet above the ground. There was nothing close enough to grab to get to the ground and after struggling for a while he pulled the ripcord on his reserve, dropped it to the ground like a rope ladder and got out of his harness and slid down the reserve to mother earth. He'd lost the flashlight in the process and groped through he woods for another hour until he found the road and flagged down the guy who had given him the ride.

Though we had been keeping what we had done under wraps until Curt appeared everyone in the place now knew the whole story so our cover was blown but we were relieved that he was alive and really didn't give a shit. We staggered out at closing time and went to the house in Athol for a couple of home brews.

Two weeks later a registered letter with the return address of the Massachusetts Aeronautics Commission arrived at the Center informing me that I was not to make a parachute jump in the state of Massachusetts for the next sixty days because I had participated in an unauthorized night jump. I never found out who blew the whistle. Probably a local from Mike's or possibly a jumper from Orange that I'd grounded for some infraction. They didn't fine me and the grounding was a minor penalty that I was going to ignore anyway so I figured that the bureaucracy determined that their evidence was weak and that was the most they could do. They didn't know who the other jumpers were and I thought that Nate was off the hook but the FAA caught up with him a month or so later and suspended him for a month, which he too, dutifully ignored.

I keep the suspension letter framed in my office so I can show the new kids that I wasn't always a conservative old fart.

Chapter 7

I'm Not Jake

In the summer of 1965 Jake and I were caught up in separate incidents that were similar, were somewhat life threatening, and involved women. Other men's women.

Mine happened at Orange and to avoid further trouble we'll call the other party Jane, a tall brunette with bedroom eyes and a killer figure. She was married to a jumping regular and had made a few herself, but she usually just hung around the airport while her old man was jumping and partied with us in the evenings. I had the hots for her but always tried to avoid eating another guy's porridge.

Jane, and we'll call him Bill, were always having tiffs that blew over in a couple of days but this time it seemed serious and she moved out of the house and was staying with a girlfriend in the area. Nate and I ran into them at the Inn on a Saturday night and he swooped on her girlfriend while Jane cried on my shoulder about what a prick her husband was and said that this was it and she was getting a divorce. I really felt sorry for her and didn't have any carnal intentions. I usually prefer blondes, but after a couple of hours drinking cut-a-ways she started getting awfully friendly and Nate and I ended up taking Jane and her girlfriend back to the house.

We ended up in my bed just fooling around and laughing at Nate and her girlfriend bouncing off the walls in the next room. The following weekend we rented a room at the Inn and she convinced me that blondes really weren't more fun. She started spending a couple of nights a week at my place and life was good until Bill found out.

He didn't seem like the jealous type and she'd assured me that he didn't give a shit anymore, and that she was going through with the divorce, so I was surprised to hear through the Mike's Place grapevine that I was a hunted man. The word was that Bill had been following us around and that he was pissed and packing. I'm not the wimpy type but I'm not stupid either so I started keeping a lookout for Bill. Jane thought the whole thing was bullshit but he apparently was after me, not her, so I took it more seriously.

I had a gun, a twenty-five caliber Beretta that I had carried in my survival vest when I flew in the Navy and had it stashed in a back drawer in my dresser. I considered keeping it with me but started thinking about a shootout on Main Street and decided that it was a dumb idea. I hadn't cleaned or used it in years so it probably wouldn't have worked anyway.

I kept seeing Jane on and off, so to speak, for a couple of weeks but the initial sexual excitement was waning and I was getting tired of looking over my shoulder.

The end came on a Tuesday night when Nate was in Lakewood with Jill and I was home alone and sound asleep at two in the morning. I was awakened by a furious pounding at the front door. I jumped out of bed and peeked out of the bedroom window. It was raining and a dark figure in military fatigues stood at the front door with something in his hand.

I scrambled to the dresser and dug through my underwear until I found the Beretta, slid the clip into the slot and chambered a round. The banging continued as I found a flashlight and went into the living room. My hands were shaking and I kept hoping that he would give up but the banging grew louder now accompanied by muffled shouts of "Angel!"

Gun in hand, I flipped on the porch light and keeping the door between myself and the visitor, yanked it open a few inches.

"You motherfucker, I'm drowning out here," said not Bill, to my great relief, but a soaked regular jumper named Vic, just back from duty with the reserves, holding a six pack and looking for a place to crash. He looked at the gun and asked me if I was pissed that he woke me up.

A few days later I left for a two-week trip to Lakewood where I was running a jumpmaster certification course and by the time I returned Jane and Bill were back together and I was glad of it.

On that trip the Jake incident occurred. As I've mentioned, Jake was a pussy magnet, and he had very few scruples about whom he would ball. He didn't care if they were fifteen or forty, single or married, black or white. His motto was, Just Do It. He frequently had run-ins with other guys on whose territory he had been caught poaching but they usually just ended up with loud words and finger jabbing. Jake was tough but he had a killer smile and a likeable personality which usually allowed him to talk his way out of tense situations without resorting to combat, though if it was unavoidable, he threw himself in with great gusto and usually emerged the victor.

So, during the jumpmaster seminar Jake was squiring around this chick who was about ten years older than he was, kind of average looking as I recall, but she had to be good in bed or we would have only seen her once. She'd show up at the airport when her kids were in school and they'd play kissy face or hold hands in the snack bar when Jake wasn't performing his jumpmaster duties.

It looked like it might be a long-term relationship, which by Jake's standards would be about two weeks.

We were decompressing in our Lakewood bar of choice, the Red Lion, one night when Jake confided in me that his paramour's husband was suspicious and knew she had been seeing one of the jumpmasters at Lakewood named Jake, and though he didn't know what Jake looked like, was after him. I recounted my recent experience and told him not to worry about it.

Later that night, we were sitting around one of the communal houses and we started talking about Jake and the stalking husband. One thing led to another and pretty soon we were hunting for magic markers and stick-on name tags that we provided to first jumpers to avoid calling them "hey you."

The next morning everyone showed up at the airport early and lined up on flight line for our morning muster, one of Jacques military bullshit ideas. When Jake showed up the whole staff was wearing I'm Not Jake nametags with an X'd out gun in a circle below. By the following day the waitresses and busboys in the Brick luncheonette were wearing them, a day later the bartenders at the Red Lion. There was a rumor that the cuckolded husband had showed up at Lakewood and seeing the tags jumped back in his car and raced away. That may or may not be true but the rest of the story is.

Chapter 8

Time's Up

Lakewood Parachute Center opened in the spring of 1963. I still had a year left on my Navy enlistment and was stationed at the Navy Research and Development Center in Johnsville, Pa.. Lee, the manager, who I knew from my earlier days of jumping called and told me that they were building the place and asked me if I wanted a weekend job as a jumpmaster. I accepted, and because I had a lot of leave built up, took a month off to help them put the place together.

The Lakewood airport, which consisted of pinewoods and a short dirt runway had to be transformed into a state of the art parachute Center in about two months. This entailed building a three thousand foot paved runway, chopping down, clearing, burning and burying ten acres of pine trees for the drop zone and putting up three buildings.

A nearby military base was getting ready to tear down an old barracks. Jacques made a deal and had the whole thing transported to the airport where we cut it into three pieces, gutted the insides, and rebuilt them into three pretty good looking buildings for the office, classrooms and parachute loft.

Lee, an ex-Army sergeant, oversaw the operations, Connie, a jumper from Orange who was an engineer did the technical stuff, and a half dozen of us who were going to be instructing did the grunt work. The Boy not yet skydivers were there too. Fourteen or fifteen, eager to help, they constantly created more work than they ever completed.

We worked twelve-hour days and partied all night and by opening day the place looked great. We had thirty sets of the latest student and staff parachute gear, helmets with radios to talk the students down, three lumbering Norsemen and a Cessna 180.

Jacques had a lot of connections. After we opened he talked *Time* magazine into coming out to do a story on the Center.

A senior editor and his girl friend showed up for the one o'clock first jump course and I was the instructor. I was flattered to get the assignment but keenly aware that they had better have a good experience or we would look like bozos to a couple of million readers of *Time* and my career at P.I. would be severely compromised.

The writer and friend were pretty athletic and performed well during the three hour ground school so by the time we put their 'chutes on and climbed into the Norseman I felt pretty confident that the story wouldn't be featuring someone with a cast on their leg.

We took off and climbed to two grand and I threw the wind streamer, watched for two minutes until it landed and picked the opening point. There were nine students in the plane and I maneuvered the first one into the door and hooked up his static line as the pilot circled around and started jump run.

As I looked down to line up with the drop zone something caught my eye on the runway. I saw wheels sticking up in the air and then cars driving down the macadam toward the wheels. My heart sank. It was one of our airplanes; upside down, on its back. I moved the student away from the door and unhooked his static line. The pilot was now looking back over his shoulder and motioning for me to come forward to the cockpit.

I told the students to stay put and threaded my way up the narrow aisle, followed by eighteen nervous eyes. They can smell fear.

Tom, the pilot, yelled over the roaring engine that the brakes had locked on two-four-nine as he touched down and he was upside down in the middle of the runway, which I already knew. Lee wanted us to orbit while they decided what to do.

Now technically we weren't in trouble, other than the problem with the *Time* people, but we couldn't land at Lakewood until the runway was clear, and who knew when that would be.

The Norseman is a damn big airplane. Five or six strong guys can drag a Cessna out of the way but this was going to require some engineering. We had an hour of fuel left so Tom and I decided to give them twenty minutes to clear the runway before heading for the nearest airport, about twenty minutes away. I tried to tell the students what was going on but between the engine noise and the helmets they were wearing, the effort was probably futile.

The fire trucks arrived in about ten minutes followed by most of the rescue personnel in southern New Jersey to deal with a plane that wasn't on fire and the only occupant, the pilot, was standing beside the runway smoking a cigarette. From my point of view it looked like a county fair and it was time to boogie.

I got Tom's attention and pointed northeast, toward the other airport, then made sure the students had their seatbelts on. I squeezed into my seat, next to Mr. *Time*, and took his helmet off so I could yell in his ear and tell him what was happening. Things were bad enough without him thinking we were going to crash.

Monmouth County Airport was a commercial, as opposed to private, airport with a real control tower, a seven thousand foot runway and terminal building for passengers. Parachuting was an oddity then, and when we landed and the noisy Norseman with no door taxied up to the terminal and started disgorging what looked like paratroopers we quickly drew a small crowd.

Tom took the plane over to the gas pumps while I got the students out of their gear and brought them into the waiting room. The reporter seemed to be taking it well but started grilling me; what was wrong with the plane, does this happen often, how long are we going to be here, etc. I borrowed a dime from him and called the Center. They had a wrecker on the scene and were putting skids under the plane. Might be an hour and we could come back.

We retired to the coffee shop and pilot Tom fronted the money for sodas and snacks. We never carry anything in our pockets when we jump so were at his mercy. I felt guilty because that morning I'd told him that you could always recognize a pilot because they have a hangover and a hard-on and are looking for a place to cash a check.

We finally got the all-clear call and it took another forty-five minutes to 'chute everybody up and gear check them. It had been a couple hours since we'd finished the training so they had, of course, forgotten everything I'd taught them, requiring a quick refresher and a lot of hand holding.

I threw another streamer when we got back to Lakewood in case the wind had changed, and tossed the jumpers out, following the last one down to the sand bowl.

By the time we finished de-briefing and giving out first jump certificates the exhilaration of having survived the jump had pushed the airplane incident to the back of the students' minds and the subsequent magazine article filled our first jump courses for the next two years.

Though we'd been lucky that day, fate was still stalking the airport. One of the guys who helped get the Norseman off the runway took off in his own plane just before sunset and crashed in the woods. He and his passenger burned to death before we could help them.

Chapter 9

Geronimo

There was an annual event at Orange that all of us on the staff looked forward to and at the same time dreaded. I know that sounds contradictory.

There are lots of military ex-airborne chapters around the country and this one was based in Boston and most of the members were W.W.II veterans in their forties and fifties. There were lawyers, including one of the most prominent defense guys on the east coast, a priest, a couple of cops, plumbers. You get the picture.

They would start arriving on Thursday and the last stragglers would drag their bedraggled asses out of town by the following Tuesday. The meet was Saturday and Sunday and we had events like jumping with raw eggs in your hand and trying to land with them unbroken, hit and rock, with a rocking chair on the target and you're timed from when you touch down until you're in the chair rocking, and a bunch of other silly shit. The problem was they had to jump.

These guys were war heroes who had jumped in most of the big airborne invasions during the war, but that was twenty-five years ago and now they were sedentary, middle aged men with kids and a mortgage. Half of them had impressive beer guts, none of them were in good shape, and the only jumps they made were the two or three a year at Orange during the meet.

They were making static line jumps so the main 'chute was going to open automatically but they had to steer it into the landing area and land without damaging themselves. In a futile attempt to minimize casualties we required them to take a refresher course each year where we tried to teach them how to steer and do parachute landing falls. It never worked, however, because they thought by virtue of their military training from a quarter of a century ago that they knew everything. And they were usually under the influence for the entire weekend.

For obvious reasons we had strict rules about not drinking at the Center until the planes were tied down for the day. If we caught someone swigging a beer in the parking lot or got a whiff of Jack Daniels on a student's breath they had to take a rain check and make their jump another day. The 82nd was just a different situation. We knew we couldn't stop them; they were friends, and they weren't wimpy guys. If they did something stupid and hurt themselves they would slink away and lick their wounds. Nobody sued in 1965, so for one weekend a year we looked the other way.

On Saturday morning one of the instructors, the one who drew the short straw, would herd them into the classroom for the refresher. We kept them separated from our regular students because of their condition and language, which, even by our liberal standards, was shocking.

Most of them slept through the one-hour lecture and when they were outside in the training area for the practical section of the course they were always wandering off to piss or throw up in the woods or make a trip to their cars in the parking lot. By noon they were in God's hands and we started the meet. The jumpmaster would spot for them and hook their static lines up. With normal people we would watch the student leave the door and evaluate their ability to fall stable while the parachute was opening, in preparation for freefall. With the 82nd we would yell "Go" and turn our heads to avoid future nightmares as they tumbled out in an Airborne tuck, back loop, front loop, or fall through the risers as the main canopy tried to open. When it did, they ignored the radio instruction from the ground and didn't use their steering toggles to guide the parachute, instead trying to spill air by yanking on the risers the way they did in Normandy.

As I mentioned before, the drop zone at Orange was a sand bowl in the middle of a triangle of runways. If you did anything right, even it was your first jump, you could make the landing area. If you missed there were grass fields beside the runways that spread to the edge of the woods. By the time the second Norseman flight was in the air someone from the first flight was already hanging in a tree, hundreds of yards away from the bowl. Another had bounced off the macadam and was being dragged by his inflated 'chute. Ad infinitum.

We always hired extra staff on 82nd weekends. By two o'clock Saturday afternoon three or four people would be in the woods getting jumpers and parachutes out of trees, a driver would be making round trips to the emergency room ferrying the wounded there and dropping the repaired ones at Mike's on the return trip, and a couple of us helped judge the meet and followed them around to make sure that they didn't try to steal the Norseman for a joy ride or set something on fire.

As part of our containment policy we closed the Inn on Saturday night to everyone except staff and the veterans and they would proceed to get seriously fucked up. Nate would show up with a couple of cases of homebrew and we'd award trophies and sign plaster casts until dawn.

I don't know how many of the group is still around. The survivors, if any, must be in their eighties. I know that liver failure and cigarettes must have taken a heavy toll and at least a couple tried to drive through immovable objects, but you never know. Some of them may still be sitting around the VFW drinking Maalox and vodka.

Chapter 10

The Ballad of John Flood

The day that John Flood made his first jump at Orange started out badly and went downhill from there. It was a Sunday morning in the middle of July and already ninety degrees when I opened the office at 7:30. The air was heavy and damp and when I checked the weather they were forecasting heavy thunderstorms on and off through the day.

Bruce, my ground instructor, called in sick and it was too late to find a replacement, which meant that I'd be stuck out in the bowl all day talking in students. I didn't mind doing that, I enjoyed the break from my usual routine, but it meant that I would be five hundred yards from the office, the center of operations. The radio that monitored our aircraft transmissions was there and if a plane had a problem or a student landed off the airport I would immediately be aware of the situation and be able to take the proper action. There were also situations involving customers who needed refunds or were disgruntled for some reason and the girl who worked the manifest desk couldn't handle those, so I tried to stick pretty close.

The first jumpers started showing up for the ten o'clock class and I helped them register and pay. We ended up with twenty five which improved my mood and I sent them off with their instructor, Smitty, to start the course and headed down the flight line to Neva's restaurant for a sandwich and jug of iced tea to sustain me in the drop zone desert.

Neva's was not a white tablecloth restaurant. It was a small shack plunked down on the edge of the blacktopped ramp with a scenic view of the parking lot. It looked like shit; unpainted and just plain ugly. From the outside it looked uninhabitable. Inside wasn't much better.

Neva! She looked like the restaurant, unpainted and ugly. A two-hundred pound woman of undetermined age in a 1930's style Betty Crocker dress that sported soggy sweat stains in the armpits and samples of whatever she was cooking that day drizzled down the front. Whenever she smiled, which was not very often, she prominently displayed her four teeth, two on top and two on the bottom. She greeted me in her usual manner, the same as she greeted everybody.

"What do YOU want?"

As soon as I had my order I got out of there before she started in on me.

The drop zone truck was an ancient Ford pick-up that we'd given a nice white paint job with the P.I. logo on the door. Nate, the master mechanic, had replaced most of its internal organs, and even though the speedometer was on its third trip around, it fired up on the first crank. I checked for incoming planes and crossed the runway, driving through the grass and up the side of the bowl to the lip, parking next to the gear box where we kept the stuff the ground instructor needed. Fifty feet below me, deep, white sand stretched a thousand feet to the other rim. It was pretty neat.

I unlocked the equipment box and checked through the things I needed; a megaphone in case the radio crapped out, which was all the time, a first aid kit, fire extinguisher (if a plane crashed the ground instructor was closest to the runway), the radio and a telephone that sometimes allowed you to call the office. I had run the telephone wires from the office to the bowl by crawling five hundred yards through an underground pipe that was two feet in diameter and was not anxious to repeat the experience. Oh, and a few copies of *Playboy*. I guess that's why Bruce didn't mind spending the day out here by himself.

My 'chute shaggers showed up just as the first flight took off and checked in with me. They were kids in their mid-teens with pink uniform pants and P.I. t-shirts. They were a little chagrinned to find that I was going to be talking in students. They could pull a lot of shit on Bruce, who was only a couple of years older than them, but the boss was here and it was going to be a long day.

The plane dropped a streamer and the first student was a guy with five or six jumps, so I sent the shaggers into the bowl to help him with his gear when he landed and keyed the mike. I let him know I was there and let him steer himself until he was ready to land then told him to turn him into the wind. He performed a great parachute landing fall and I gave him props on the manifest sheet.

There were a few more flights before we went on wind hold as a storm with towering white cumulous clouds slid by the airport a mile or so to the south.

The first jump class didn't start to jump until four o'clock, two hours later than normal. Smitty was breaking in a new instructor, Butch, which slowed things down, and the wind hold killed another hour. The Norseman could carry nine jumpers and the pilot. Because Butch and Smitty were going up on each flight they'd have seven first jumpers on each of the first three or four flights and the last was a money-losing proposition with the plane half-empty.

I arranged the manifest sheets with the jumper's names in the proper order on my clipboard and went back to work as the first orange and white canopy blossomed. The wind started to pick up when the second flight took off and I called the office and told Linda to call the plane and tell them to throw another streamer. The sky to the southwest was getting darker but there wasn't any lightening or thunder. That meant the storm was ten miles away or more. I turned my attention to the second flight and got everybody into the bowl.

The first student on the third flight never touched his toggles and missed the bowl, landing in the grass beside the runway. One of the shaggers took off after him and I had the second guy halfway to the ground when the shit hit the fan. From my elevated position on the lip of the bowl I could see the whole airport. Three Norsemen and a Cessna were parked on the ramp in front of the office and they were all moving, not taxiing, moving in random patterns, circles, as a wall of dust came out of nowhere and engulfed the whole area. I frantically dialed the phone to the office to get the flight aborted and at the same time get the 2nd jumper down safely. I screamed at the kids to tear up the target, our backup signal to abort in case of radio failure, and looked up as John Flood made his first jump.

The wind slammed into me at seventy miles an hour and blew the equipment box over the lip of the bowl. Small pieces of grit were pelting my face and blinding me as I groped for the door handle of the truck. Inside I looked up through the windshield and caught a glimpse of Flood, already a half-mile away and gaining altitude under the twenty-eight foot round parachute.

I'm good under pressure but this was something else. I briefly considered trying to retrieve the radio which had rolled down the hill with the equipment box, but I realized that even if it still worked the antenna was down and Flood would soon be out of radio range anyway. Even if I could have talked to him it would have done no good. He was hanging under a parachute with a six mile an hour forward speed being blown away by a seventy mile an hour wind. "Hey John, this is your ground instructor. You're gonna' die." I needed to get to the office and the airplane radio.

I drove gingerly along the lip of the bowl and saw the shaggers and the two students that had landed hunkered down behind the upwind side so I continued down and across the runway to the flight line. The wall of dust had dissipated and I jumped out of the truck and looked up as Flood's canopy, now a tiny dot in the distance, headed for the Quabbin reservoir, the largest body of water in Massachusetts, a few miles to the south.

The airplanes were scattered around the ramp like toys, a wingtip ripped off of one and another impaled by a two by four that stuck out of it's fabric skin like a dagger. The ground was littered with the contents of trashcans that were now rolling down the runway, two hundred yards away. I dashed into the office and grabbed the mike from Linda.

Ed was flying and I asked him how much fuel he had. The next closest airport was a half hour away and I didn't know how long the storm would last. There was no way they could land at Orange.

Smitty was a stocky little guy from Illinois and a good friend of mine. We had been in the Navy together, flying off of carriers in the Med, and had been discharged around the same time as me. I taught him how to jump and gave him a job as a jumpmaster when he was qualified. Smitty was a smart guy and had a lot of balls. If I couldn't be up in the plane he was the one I'd pick.

Smitty told me that they were following Flood in the plane. He had been moving away from the airport at fifty miles an hour and had been sucked up to six thousand feet by the up-drafts and was heading dead on for the reservoir. I told Smitty to stay with him and try to give us a good fix when he landed so we could get the rescue teams there.

I went outside and the wind was gone. The black sky was to the east and sun was starting to break through in the west. People started emerging from where they'd taken shelter, shaken and unsmiling. I sent someone out to the bowl to retrieve the kids and student jumpers and mustered the staff in the office. Everyone was inclined to head for the Quabbin but until we knew where he landed it would be futile to try to comb thousands of acres of woods and water with a few people. We decided to sit tight and monitor the situation on the radio. I called the cops again and gave them the frequency the plane was on to help coordinate the search. John Flood was now six miles away and over the water at five thousand feet. Smitty told me that they were flying right beside him and they'd stay with him until he landed. He didn't tell me everything. Ed called back in five minutes and told me that Smitty and Butch weren't there anymore. They'd jumped.

I almost emptied my bladder. No one said anything.

The plane was still in the windstorm that had blown through the airport and Smitty and Butch jumped out to follow Flood down. If he went in the water he wouldn't have a chance of getting out of the heavy student gear he was wearing. Float time was about three minutes until the parachutes became a wet anchor. Smitty and

Butch could be out of their rigs as soon as they hit the water and help Flood get free, and hopefully to shore. Dicey but possible.

The cops called back and told us they were at the reservoir and talking to the plane. It was going to be dark in an hour.

When Smitty and Butch opened right beside Flood he must have felt like Batman and Robin had arrived. About a mile down the body of water the three jumpers got out of the updrafts and started descending at a normal rate, though clipping along at forty miles an hour. The wind saved them. At two thousand feet they were over land again and drifted into a valley between two fifteen hundred foot hills, on the far side of the reservoir. The landings weren't pretty, but survivable. The hills blocked a lot of the wind and they landed in a thick pine woods seven miles from the airport.

Butch cracked a rib and Smitty had a few cuts. John Flood was fine. The cops got to them just before dark and we were getting John drunk at the Inn by nine o'clock.

Chapter 11

Sail Wing

In 1965 an inventor/engineer named Dave Barish showed up at Lakewood with a radical new parachute that he'd designed called the Sail Wing. At that time most jumpers were jumping surplus military parachutes with holes cut in them to give the jumper forward speed and the ability to turn left or right. Most of us had a sport version of these 'chutes made out of low porosity material for softer landings and better control and there were a few Para Commanders being jumped which were still round but more hi-tech than Lo-Po's.

The Sail Wing was a completely different animal. If you can picture a giant bra for a three-breasted woman you'll get the idea. Rather than being a cargo-retarding device like the round parachutes, the jumper being the cargo, the Sail Wing was built to perform like an aircraft wing. It had a tremendous forward speed when flying flat out, probably thirty miles an hour, and could be slowed to zero for landing by pulling both steering toggles down, which is called braking. The inventor, Barish, wanted the P.I. staff, who were the most experienced jumpers on the east coast, to test jump and help develop it.

We initially did test drops with Stan, a 150-pound wooden dummy who had unfortunately lost his arms and legs in some drunken mishap, no doubt involving the Boy Skydivers. Stan would be put in a harness, the parachute attached, then be static lined out of the Norseman. Half of the time the Wing would fail to open and streamer into the landing area at a high rate of speed, blasting sand twenty feet in the air, to the great amusement of the 'chute shaggers. Whenever it did open, Stan, with no arms, couldn't steer and it would fly erratically into the power lines, woods, or Leisure Village, increasing the already high heart attack rate of the elderly inmates that populated the development. So, we decided to start jumping it.

Despite the brilliant overall concept, the Sail Wing had some major flaws. The material it was made of was like nylon sailcloth with a chemical coating that was rolled on under high pressure making it non-porous. When a jumper was falling at terminal velocity and pulled the ripcord the opening shock was so severe that he was in danger of ending up like Stan. We also didn't know if the material would withstand a terminal opening despite Barish's assurance that it would. Nate and Lee made the first couple of jumps with it; hop and pops with just a three second freefall. The success rate was the same as the Stan drops. Half the time it opened and half the time they came down on their reserves. When it opened though, it was ultra cool. Regardless of the wind you could cruise around at triple the speed of the Lo-Po's and P.C.'s that we thought were high tech at the time. When it was time to land you could fly it in like an airplane on a long final approach into the wind and use the steering brakes to stall just as you touched down, with a tiptoe landing in the center of the target.

I finally talked Barish into letting me have a shot at it. Nate and Lee had been stretching the freefall to five or six seconds and we'd been wrapping a length of clothesline around the suspension lines when we packed the Wing to slow down the opening.

I made a couple of hop and pops and had good openings. After a thousand jumps on the slow, round chutes I knew that this was the future. It really was like flying an airplane. I was pumped and decided to try a longer freefall, maybe eight seconds, eighty miles an hour on opening, well short of terminal at one-twenty.

I was wearing a bulky, quilted flight suit that I'd stolen from the Navy and heavy gloves. I put a couple of static line students out of the Norseman and yelled at the pilot to take me up to five grand. I wanted to open at four thousand rather than the normal two thousand to have extra time to deal with any problems I might encounter when I pulled the ripcord.

I had the pilot do a few left and right corrections as we flew over the drop zone, pushed the cut button, and hopped out. My goggles fogged over from the cold but I was counting off the freefall anyway so I wasn't worried about looking at my altimeter. When I reached eight I felt for the ripcord, which was buried in the folds of the bulky flight suit. I yanked my goggles off and took another few seconds to find it but was now head-down and had to rotate back to a flat and stable position before I pulled. I was now past terminal velocity and I braced myself for a killer opening shock. I gritted my teeth as the pilot 'chute caught air and I felt the deployment bag lift off my back. To my amazement I was pulled gently into an upright position as the Sail Wing opened. "Well, that wasn't so bad," I thought and looked up to check the canopy. Most of it wasn't there, at least not recognizable as a parachute. The high-speed opening had blown it to pieces. Some ripped remnants of material were trailing from the suspension lines and some were literally floating up and away as my rate of descent, slowed momentarily by the explosion above my head, rapidly increased. It was time to leave the accident scene. I ripped off my gloves and grabbed the covers of my cape wells on each shoulder and popped the covers. The cutaway rings popped out and I inserted my thumbs and gave a simultaneous yank as my altimeter passed twenty five hundred.

Back in freefall I rolled on my back and pulled the belly mount reserve ripcord. Because it's your last option, the reserve always seems like it's taking forever to open. When the reserve finally yanked me upright I looked down and saw that I was already downwind of the drop zone and under the non-steerable twenty-eight foot 'chute I was just along for the ride. Two minutes later I crashed through a stand of pines trees a hundred yards short of the Garden State Parkway and lay on the ground cursing Barish, and myself for letting the freefall go too long.

A month or so later Barish re-appeared with a couple of new Wings made out of different material. He seemed to have forgiven me for destroying the other 'chute and asked me to demonstrate the Wing for a group of Army brass who were coming up to Lakewood from the Pentagon the following Wednesday. I was flattered that he'd asked me and determined to give them a good show.

When I got out of bed the morning of the jump my house was shaking. I looked out the window and saw the willow tree in my yard trying to take off and anything that wasn't tied down flying up the street. Bummer!

I took a shower and got to the airport around nine. Barish was already there waiting for me and said that the Army guys were on the way. The jump was scheduled for noon.

I called flight service and the forecast was for twenty to thirty knots with higher gusts all day.

While we packed the rig Barish kept telling me that I didn't have to make the jump if I didn't think it was safe, but I think it was just for liability reasons. He'd been trying to get money for development from the military, promoting the idea that Special Forces could use the Sail Wing for special-ops and it could be jumped under almost any conditions, including high winds. He didn't have to talk me into doing it. I wasn't going to be the wimpy asshole to stand there in front of a bunch of generals and say I was afraid to jump in a little wind.

If the parachute opened, I was sure I could get it into the drop zone and wouldn't get hurt in the sand even if the landing was a little rough. The problem was that from its track record, there was a fifty-fifty chance that it wouldn't open and I'd be landing who knew where in a non-steerable reserve traveling thirty miles an hour. I'd crashed and burned a lot of times since I started jumping and had never broken anything but there's a first time for everything.

The Brass pulled in around twelve-thirty; two black limos with little general flags flying from the front bumpers. There were four officers, a half dozen aides and a photographer. We bullshitted for a few minutes as the wind ripped through the pines and sand blasted the flight line. I got into my gear as Tom, our weekday pilot, fired up the Cessna and taxied over to pick me up. The wind was, luckily, down the runway. If there had been a cross wind we'd have never gotten off the ground and I was thinking that no matter how bad the jump might be I was glad I didn't have to land in the plane with Tom.

Sometimes when the ground winds are strong, the winds aloft are moderate or even light but this wasn't the case. I was kneeling on the floor holding onto the seat belt like a rodeo bull rider to keep from being slammed into the overhead as Tom fought up and down drafts. We climbed to four thousand feet and I threw the wind streamer. Within thirty seconds it had passed the dry lakes, crossed the Parkway and was almost out of sight. Normally after the streamer lands you take the distance it lands downwind and transpose it upwind in a straight line to arrive at the point that you should get out of the plane. The steamer was out of sight before it was even close to the ground. I opted for plan B. Fly upwind for a couple of miles and get the hell out. If the Wing worked I could deal with it, if it didn't I was screwed anyway and it didn't matter where I landed.

I poked my head out of the door and looked down. Our airspeed read eighty knots but we couldn't have been moving across the ground at more than thirty. The town of Lakewood was about three miles upwind and that was where I decided to exit. I had Tom drop down to three thousand. If the Wing opened I wouldn't have any trouble getting back to the drop zone and if I had to open my reserve I wanted to make sure I didn't drift past the airport where there were power lines, the Parkway, Atlantic Ocean, and if the wind got much stronger, England.

Not putting much faith in Barish's assurances about the new canopy material I pulled right off of the step and was rewarded with a beautiful, fully inflated Sail Wing. Life was good.

I un-stowed the steering lines and turned down wind. The airport was barely in sight, three miles away, but it wasn't going to take long to get there. Looking down at the suburbs streaming past my toes I figured I was traveling about sixty miles an hour, the thirty-mile an hour parachute speed plus the thirty or more wind speed behind me.

I ran with the wind until I was at five hundred feet and a few hundred yards upwind of the landing area where I made a turn into the wind and checked my drift, just a few miles an hour backwards.

The small knot of spectators were huddled on the lollipop turnaround at the end of the road from the Center to the drop zone, a few yards from the white X that I was aiming for.

I slowly backed toward the target until I was a hundred and fifty feet from the ground and whipped a three hundred and sixty degree turn and touched down fifty feet from the target. I grabbed my capewells and cut the canopy away before it dragged me away from my fans. I was Master of the Universe, or at least the Sail Wing, so I thought.

About a year later I was back at Orange and had about eighty jumps on the parachute, half of them malfunctions. Because we had so many reserve openings we had started jumping with two reserve 'chutes, one on the back in a piggyback rig that had just hit the market, and another in the front. All of us who were jumping the Wing were getting nervous about going to our last 'chute that many times. It was only a matter of time before the odds caught up with us and someone would have a reserve malfunction and bounce.

It was the dead of winter and I was making another test jump, wearing everything I could put on and two pair of gloves. I got out at four thousand and pulled at the count of five. Before I even looked up I started spinning and was pissed at the thought of landing on my reserve on the frozen ground. One of the three lobes of the Wing was inverted and I was spinning so fast that I was horizontal to the ground. It wasn't the first time that I'd encountered this type malfunction and on a couple of other occasions I'd been able to climb up the lines enough to flip the inverted wing right side out and get the parachute flying again, thus averting a cutaway.

Keeping an eye on my altimeter, I climbed hand over hand until I was almost within reach of the problem lobe. By now I was getting dizzy from the spin and my arms felt like they were being pulled out of their sockets. I lost my grip and as I slid back down the suspension lines several of them wrapped around my right wrist immobilizing my arm.

I was passing through two thousand feet by then and had to get rid of the main 'chute. If I opened my reserve with the other spinning parachute out there the odds were excellent that the two would become entangled. My problem was that I needed two hands to pull the cutaway rings that would release my main. I was trying to think fast and wondered if it's true what they say about pot screwing up your memory and reflexes.

I carry a hook knife on my chest strap, designed for cutting through parachute lines and webbing, designed exactly for my present dilemma. I yanked it out of the sheath and ripped through the lines that were wrapped around my wrist. The last one gave way at twelve hundred feet and I dug my thumbs in the capewell rings and jettisoned the spinning main, pulling the reserve ripcord a second later. After a thirty second canopy ride I landed, of course, on the runway, which probably wasn't much harder than the ground at that time of year.

That was about the end of the Sail Wing project. It never got to the manufacturing stage and other competing designs became the modern square parachutes. To those of us who got to test jump it then it was like space flight, half terror and half ecstasy.

Chapter 12

Tee

Back in the dark ages, when I was a child, my father taught me to stand on my head. He was a steel worker who was often on rotating shifts, which meant that two thirds of the time he was working or sleeping in the evenings and we didn't see much of him. When he worked days or was off we would roughhouse on the living room floor and he'd teach me tricks, which I still use to bore or amuse my fans.

When I moved into the house in Athol with Nate I discovered that he was also a head standing aficionado. If you've never tried it you may not appreciate the balance and arm strength required to stay inverted for long periods of time. It only takes a minor movement of a foot to displace your center of gravity and send you tumbling backwards onto a favorite glass coffee table or in our case, a recycled orange crate.

So Nate and I, on slow nights at home, developed our head standing technique and eventually became quite proficient. We initially used a stopwatch to time each other's inverted performance but got bored with that and designed a game to make it more interesting.

Part of our décor was a naked 100-watt light bulb that hung just above head height in the middle of the kitchen. We attached a piece of parachute suspension line to the pull chain and adjusted the length so that we could grasp it between our feet while standing on our head and turn it on and off, competing for the most cycles.

Now this may sound stupid but after a few home brews or other reflex impairing substances, it was quite challenging. The linoleum floor was brutal on your head and the movement of your legs to grasp and pull the string to turn the light on and off made it very difficult to maintain balance. We considered using a pillow to pad our head but decided that it was wimpy and continued to suffer for our art.

We were up to about sixty or seventy cycles each. The title would shift back and forth between us, depending who was the most impaired at the time. Then we started performing for visitors. A party would be raging around us. Throughout the house the Ten Commandments were being broken with great gusto, (except for stealing), and Nate and I would be red-faced and upside down while a circle of guests counted off our attempts. Of course others then wanted to try and we'd deride their pitiful attempts at fifteen or twenty cycles before they toppled into the crowd and slunk off into another room.

I must admit that we had a home court advantage. The challengers were only there for a night once in a while and didn't have the benefit of a hanging light bulb in their more conventional domiciles. We could practice a lot and played a couple of rounds almost every night during our most compulsive period.

We'd probably still be playing the game today if it hadn't been for the U.S. Team. Not light turning off team, Parachute Team. They were at Orange for a competition; I think it was the Governor's Cup, an annual meet that drew the best style and accuracy jumpers from the east coast to compete for trophies. Several members of both the men and women's team were there, just back from the world meet in Europe.

After jumping all-day and hitting the bars we ended up back at the house and Nate and I started our routine. I did seventy-five and he beat me by a few before we turned the playing field over to the guests. The guys weren't very impressive. As good as they were in freefall they only made it into the fifties before collapsing. Then Tee wanted to play. She had just won the world championship in style and accuracy.

We'd never had a female in the game and I don't know if she'd ever stood on her head before.

It took her a couple of tries to get the balance right but when she did, she kicked our ass. We stopped counting after a hundred and she only stopped because she had to take a piss.

Chapter 13

Judy

While I'm on the subject of women jumpers I have to tell you about Judy's water jump.

I actually knew Judy at another parachute Center in New Jersey before I went to work for P.I. The place was called Tri-State and was in the middle of the state near Princeton. It was owned and managed by a guy named George, an ex-Army Ranger with one leg and a bad attitude. George would take off his plastic leg before he got in the airplane for a jump and whichever staff member was on the shit list that week would have to take it out to the drop zone so he could put it on when he landed. It was an unpleasant task on a hot day when the aroma from his sweaty stump would permeate your nostrils as you schlepped it a few hundred yards from the runway to the target. I tried to stay on his good side.

To qualify for a Class "D" Parachutist license, the highest, it was required that among other things such as two hundred jumps, a certain amount of freefall time and passing a written test, that you had to make a water jump. The rationale being that you could teach student jumpers how to survive an accidental water landing. Judy had all of her other qualifications and one hot day in July showed up with her bathing suit and water wings.

There was, conveniently, a small lake/pond a few hundred yards from the runway that we used for these occasional jumps but mostly for skinny-dipping after the day's jumping was over. It covered a couple of acres and was probably ten feet deep in the middle which fulfilled the Parachute Club of America requirements that qualifying jumps be made into a body of water deep enough to drown in. Badly put I thought.

I gave her a review of procedures and she insisted that I come on the flight to make sure that she got out in the right place and didn't miss the lake. We had a bunch of students to deal with that day and I wasn't anxious to waste time going up to baby sit her on the jump, nor see her in a bathing suit, but nice guy that I am, I capitulated.

She was bitching about the wind and other crap as we boarded the Cessna and started down the runway. Nerves. She insisted on spotting which was what she had dragged me along to do, and told me to just double check.

We threw the streamer and it showed the exit point to be a well defined field about three hundred yards upwind of the lake. I made doubly sure she knew exactly where to get out and told the pilot to start jump run.

Judy was kneeling on the floor with her head out in the slipstream, giving the pilot corrections with her thumb as I knelt behind her, doggy style, and looked out over her shoulder. We got to a point where Judy should be climbing out and I tapped her on the shoulder and pointed to the step. She shook her head and kept looking down. I tapped her harder and pointed again. She shook her head again. We were now past the exit point and I slapped her hard on the butt and pushed her part way out the door. She turned and looked at me through the goggle covered coke bottle glasses she wore and at a snail's pace worked her way out onto the step. I looked down and figured that if she left at that second she had a chance to make it back downwind to the lake.

After screaming "go" a couple of times I knew it was too late. I grabbed her harness to pull her back into the cockpit to make another pass when she jumped, almost pulling me out of the plane with her.

She was supposed to freefall for five seconds but she did ten, making matters worse because she was now not only too long she was too low. No chance to make the lake where the safety crew floated around in a leaky rowboat waiting for her.

There were only a few trees on the upwind side of the lake and she carefully steered herself into a fifty footer that was unfortunately dead and leafless. Landing in a tree with leaves on it is not too bad. The leaves cushion the impact and protect your body from sharp branches. Dead trees are a bitch. You're going to get chopped up, particularly in a bathing suit.

We circled and saw the boat guys' row to shore and run after her. I briefly considered going out to help after we landed but thought better of it. Maybe she'd cool down by the time she got back to the drop zone. Nah!

She was still yelling obscenities when they brought her back a half hour later, bleeding from a plethora of cuts and a three-foot hole ripped in her favorite parachute. When she asked me why she missed the lake I swallowed my answer (stupidity), and just shrugged. People were running in all directions to find a place to explode with laughter without her seeing them.

To Judy's credit, after some first aid, she borrowed a parachute and went back and hit the lake on her second attempt. I missed it because I chickened out and left for the day before she landed.

Chapter 14

Nick

Nick was a jumper at Lakewood who wanted to break the world record for the highest parachute jump. That wasn't going to be easy because in 1958 an army captain named Joe Kittinger had jumped from 102,000 feet in gloves and boots that were attached to his pressure suit with duct tape.

Kittinger jumped from a balloon and plummeted fifteen miles with only a small drogue 'chute to stabilize his body until he opened his main parachute at 18,000 feet. He was lucky to survive with only a mild case of frostbite.

Nick, a truck driver who lived in Lakewood, was shooting for 120,000 feet or higher, about the limit of balloon technology in those days. He had to jump from a balloon because there were no planes that could reach that altitude then, and still aren't.

One of the main obstacles that he faced was financing. He didn't have the hundred grand or so that was needed to pay for the balloon, ground crew, spacesuit, and telemetry that was needed but he was a great bull-shitter and he ended up getting most of the stuff donated and found a few backers including Jacques, owner of P.I., and Pioneer Parachute Company who put up the money for the rest.

I was interested in the project because it was cool and I had also made a much more modest jump from 21,000 feet a few years earlier which was the New Jersey record for quite a while. Anyway, Nick was making practice jumps at Lakewood, learning to freefall in the space suit with about a hundred pounds of other equipment; parachutes, oxygen, survival gear and recording devices.

I made some camera jumps with him, documenting his practice jumps on film for a planned movie of the jump and shooting stills for the promotion.

In October 1965, Nick took off from New Brighton, Minnesota in a balloon containing almost 4,000,000 cubic feet of helium. He rapidly ascended to 22,000 feet and was over St. Paul when a wind shear, not uncommon, ripped the fragile fabric and the balloon and gondola fell toward the city. Nick stayed in the gondola until 10,000 feet before bailing out to be able to steer his parachute to a safe landing area, which turned out to be the city dump.

Raven Industries were the primo big balloon guys in the world with a lot of experience building and launching high altitude experiments for the government and the military. Nick had gotten them on board and was going to make the second attempt in Sioux Falls, South Dakota, where Raven had their plant and launch facility. The jump was planned for the dead of winter for a couple of reasons. The land around the launch facility was flat, open farmland for a hundred miles. By the time the balloon reached jump altitude it would drift a long distance and Nick didn't want to take a chance on landing in a mountainous area or a large city.

Another potential problem was water. The land was flat and open but dotted with lakes and rivers. If he landed in water with all the equipment that he was strapped to he'd be toast. In the middle of winter everything would be frozen and snow covered, eliminating that hazard. The third consideration was inflation. Reaching the altitude that he was attempting would depend on the expansion of gas in the balloon as the sun heated it. Filling the balloon in the coldest possible conditions would allow more gas to be pumped in and more subsequent expansion as he ascended, making a higher altitude possible.

Nick would be riding in a telephone booth sized gondola suspended beneath the three hundred foot balloon. He'd be wired to body sensors that measured heartbeat, respiration, and other vital signs that would alert the ground crew to signs of trouble. If he were to encounter a medical problem that would incapacitate him, Nick, and the gondola could be released from the balloon and descend on an emergency parachute.

The gondola was unheated and the temperature at 100,000 feet would be as much as a hundred below zero, but in a full pressure suit the cold wouldn't affect him.

The second attempt was in February 1966. The balloon was inflated by the Raven crew and Nick squeezed his two hundred pound frame into the tiny gondola and launched at noon. Two hours later he was at 123,500 feet, the highest man had ever ascended in a balloon. Before he could jump he had to unhook the hose that connected him to the gondola's oxygen tank and transfer to his personal oxygen system that would provide suit pressurization and breathing during the freefall. But the hose connection was frozen.

Nick struggled with the frozen valve. He needed a wrench but had no tools aboard. He and the head of the ground crew were down to the last option. They would release the gondola from the balloon and freefall it and Nick to an altitude where the recovery parachute would open and bring the gondola and Nick to safety. He braced himself as the ground crew fired the release and the gondola accelerated to six hundred miles an hour as it plummeted toward earth. Nick used the last of his physical resources to keep from falling out of the gondola, which was open on one side. If he fell out the oxygen hose would rip off depressurizing his suit and cause instant death.

The parachute opened just below 10,000 feet and fifteen minutes later he smashed into a soybean field and emerged battered but alive and waited for the rescue crew. He decided to try again.

Three months later, in May, he launched from Sioux Falls again. He had reached 57,000 feet when he shouted "Emergency" over the intercom. The ground crew again cut the gondola away from the balloon and it began a thirty-minute parachute descent. By the time they reached him he was unconscious, having been without oxygen for the entire descent.

It was never clear whether his suit failed or as one of the crew surmised, he experienced an embolism and tried to momentarily vent pressure by opening his suit visor a crack in an effort to clear it.

He remained in a coma and died five months later.

Nick's attempts stayed on my mind for the next few years and despite the tragic outcome I felt that the high jump was possible. With my friend Frank, a jumpmaster at Orange, we put together the Stratospheric Freefall Project, an attempt to jump from a balloon from 150,000 feet.

The first person to join the team was Jeff Hoffman, a friend from Boston who was a graduate student in astronomy at MIT. Jeff and his brother, Bob, had learned to skydive at Orange when they were in their late teens and spent a few nights crashing and partying at my house in Athol on weekends.

Frank and I were confident that we would be able to make the jump but we didn't have the resources or engineering background to mathematically prove that the free fall would be survivable.

Frank had completed his work for a Doctorate in biology and I was a high school graduate who'd always sucked at math and physics. Jeff was brilliant and had access to the computer facilities at MIT, which in 1969 probably had the computing power of an I-pod, but then again so did the Lunar Lander.

A couple of weeks later we met in Orange and Jeff had a stack of information; graphs and charts, mathematical formulas, temperature data, and his opinion was that it could be done but it wasn't going to be easy.

In the first minute of free fall we would fall 60,000 feet and accelerate to just a little over mach two. The temperature at jump altitude would be sixty below zero and total free fall time would be a little under four minutes, opening our parachutes at fifteen thousand feet. The weight of our equipment, including pressure suits, oxygen equipment, parachutes, and cameras would be close to a hundred pounds. Gulp!

I called Ed Yost, the top high altitude balloon guy at Raven Industries in Sioux Falls. Ed had been in charge of building Nick's balloons and was probably one of the most experienced in the world in his field. He was interested and I sent him Jeff's data to prove that we were serious and he got back to me in a couple of weeks. Raven could build the balloon that we'd need to get us thirty miles high. It would take a couple of months and cost around twenty grand. They would also provide the telemetry, communications and ground crew for the launch in Sioux Falls.

I started promoting and fundraising and Frank started lining up oxygen equipment, parachute gear (we had parachutes of our own, of course, but we would need larger canopies to carry the increased weight of our extra equipment), and pressure suits. I contacted film companies and magazines who might be interested in buying the rights to the project and finally got an offer from *Time* for a cover story for $10,000 and enough commitments from other magazines and film companies to cover most of the cost.

In March of 1970 my son was born which led to some reflection on the gravity of what we were trying to do. I thought of Nick, who lay in a coma, wasting away for five months before he died. I thought of all the uncontrollable things that might occur and all the unknowns involved in something that no one had ever done, the mistakes that we might make, the price that we might pay. If we were successful we would have made the highest parachute jump, hold the world's highest balloon flight record, make the longest free fall, and travel faster than any human alive without the use of a machine. I thought it was worth it.

I was close to Nick's attempts and knew the mistakes that he made. We wouldn't make them. I had survived hundreds of carrier landings, a couple of airplane crashes, a mid-air collision in a jet bomber, a lightning strike in a plane, and lots of hairy parachute test jumps. I was fatalistic and confident but not stupid.

We could do this. By the summer Frank had lined up most of the equipment we needed except for the pressure suits. Once we had them we could give Raven a deposit and they'd start on the balloon. There were three sources for the suits; the U.S.

Government, the suit manufacturer ILC Industries, or the Russians. I guess you could say two sources. The Cold War and the space race eliminated the prospect of the Russians. We wasted a lot of time negotiating with our government bureaucracy and though we had some promising contacts, it turned out to be a dead end, which left ILC, the suit manufacturer. It only took a couple of phone calls and we had a commitment to provide two suits for nothing in return, except the publicity. I sent them our technical data and they were satisfied that we probably wouldn't get killed and if we did it wouldn't be the fault of the suits. They said that they had to clear a few things and get back to us.

After some anxious waiting we got the call. It seems that there was a problem. ILC was the only supplier of suits for the space program. The government had an exclusivity clause in their contract for the purpose of keeping the technology from the Russians. They couldn't give us the suits and jeopardize their contract. We called the government and kept talking to ILC, who really wanted us to use the suits, but in the end it was the death of SFFP.

In the fall of 2012, Felix Baumgartner successfully completed a jump from 127,000 feet, setting records for the highest balloon flight, longest free fall, and the fastest man has traveled without the use of a machine, more than six hundred miles per hour. Yeah Felix!

Chapter 15

The Quabbin Reservoir Disaster

The Quabbin Reservoir disaster took place in the summer of 1969. If you read the chapter about John Flood you've heard of the Quabbin, but in case you're skipping around, the Quabbin was formed by flooding the Swiftwater Valley and completed in 1943. It covers 39 square miles and supplies water to the city of Boston. Under the clear blue water lay the former towns of Dana, Enfield, Prescott, and Greenwich in addition to farms and roads, acquired in one way or another by the Massachusetts District Commission for the greater good of the masses. The pine covered foothills of the Berkshire Mountains confine the reservoir and all in all it's a very pretty place. The surface is dotted with sandy islands that support a few trees and scrub brush. One island on the north end of the reservoir, the scene of the crime, has an unusual feature; a road that appears from the water's depths on one end, slithers a thousand feet across the sand and plunges back down the side of the underwater mountain. The road is narrow, maybe thirty feet wide, and straight for two thirds of its length before bending thirty degrees.

This road to nowhere, though still intact, had suffered from lack of maintenance for the last fifty years or so, and is riddled with cracks and one humongous pothole near the curve. Why am I telling you this? You'll see. But I have to tell you something else about Nate first.

When it was raining or snowing or too windy to jump, the staff and any customers who were hanging around the parachute center would often gather in the classroom and watch 8mm home movies. Not wife and kid movies. Stuff like jumpers making crash landings, airplane crashes, and parties. Nate strapped a camera on the nose wheel of his Cessna 170 and started playing fighter pilot over the Quabbin. He'd start at six or seven thousand feet and dive toward the reservoir or the pine trees pulling out at the last minute. The effect was similar to an Imax roller coaster ride. When he wiped out the camera lens in the top of a pine tree pulling out of a dive a little late and landed back at the airport with branches stuck in the landing gear he eased off and looked for something else to amuse himself. That's when he got the idea to land on the island. It was perfect. The idea had everything; it was illegal, it was dangerous (the road was barely long enough to land and take off from), and you could bring girls out there and seduce them. So he did.

Nate was always too busy to go to the island on weekends when he was flying jumpers, instructing, and fixing airplanes, so during the week if things were slow, or on Tuesdays, our one day off, Nate would taxi off in the 170 for an afternoon delight on a deserted island. I thought it was really creative. He seldom mentioned that he went out there, but in Orange everybody knows everything eventually.

Around the first of June Nate started making plans for a party to be held on the 9th of that month. That would be 6-9-69. Nate's Class "D" expert parachutist license was D-69. It was his favorite number. He had qualified for one of the first couple of Ds' issued by the US Parachute Association but requested that they skip up to his preferred number and they granted his request. This day would never come around again and it was an occasion for a special party. He told the key players about the event but didn't tell anyone where it was going to be and told them to keep their mouths shut about the whole thing.

A couple of days before the 9th he started making mysterious flights in his 170, loading bags and boxes into the plane and disappearing for an hour or two. You know where he was going.

When the day came the Center closed around five and when everyone except those invited had left the airport Nate began ferrying people to the island. The stash of supplies that he'd brought out previously were recovered, a fire built, and copious quantities of adult beverages began flowing down dusty throats. The last group to arrive flew out in the PI 180 and jumped over the island from seven thousand feet, freefalling for thirty seconds as the sun began to set. A perfect start to a perfect evening. Right?

The 180 was flown by one of the jump Center pilots named Ed. He had been invited to the party but declined saying he had to do his laundry. Ed was a little unusual; tall and thin, with thick glasses and a lot of knees and elbows. He was a good guy and not a bad pilot but he couldn't hold a candle to Nate in that department. Ed was not supposed to land at the party. The 180 was a heavier plane than Nate's 170 and required more runway to land and take off. But Ed decided to land and he did. He stopped before he got to the water, missed the pothole, and didn't run off the narrow runway. Everyone was impressed.

The party was now in full swing, darkness was approaching, and Ed now made a fateful decision. Unless he wanted to spend the night on the island with this bunch of drunks, he would have to take off before it was too dark.

The runway/road was bad enough in the daytime but the odds of Ed making a successful take-off in the dark were slim to none.

Skip and Ken had re-packed their parachutes after jumping into the party and climbed into the plane with Ed to make another jump on his way out. He fired up the engine and swung the nose around into a light north wind, jammed the throttle to full power and rocketed down the road, the pothole six hundred feet ahead.

Remember the two pothole options? Around or straddle. Straddling is better but requires you to be precise, so the pothole is between your wheels. Going around means losing speed and there's the soft sand on the edge of the road. Ed decided to go around.

His right main wheel slipped off of the blacktop and dug into the sand at seventy miles an hour. Ground loop city.

The onlookers gasped as the plane started to spin, wingtip hitting the ground, horrible engine sound as the prop chewed into the earth at twenty six hundred rpm's. Slam bang, crash. Holy Shit!

Everyone raced down the road to the scene of the crash, trying not to spill their beer as they ran. Ken was sitting closest to the door and crawled out of the wreckage first, his head bobbing up and down, yelling "FUCK" and dusting himself off. Skip and Ed followed. Skip was probably more rattled than the other two because besides being a jumper and instructor he was an excellent jump pilot himself and had to watch Ed lose the plane and not be able to do anything about it. But except for a few cuts and bruises everyone was intact.

The partygoers weren't the only witnesses to the crash. Four hundred yards away, on the mainland, several fishermen started yelling inquiries concerning the fate of the crew but they were too far away to be understood as were the reply's of the responders. But the cat was out of the bag.

Everybody opened another beer and waited for Armageddon, standing around the remains of the 180, kicking the dirt and working on a plausible lie to lay on the authorities.

It took about an hour for the MDC cops to be notified, launch their boats, and take the beachhead with little resistance. The evidence was everywhere in the form of empty beer cans and whisky bottles, litter (sorry Arlo), and of course the remains of Jacque's airplane. There was just no place to hide anything, especially the plane. At least in their haste the MDC cops forgot that yellow crime scene tape that they could have wrapped around the island like that Christo bullshit. The boats ferried everyone back to shore where half of the police cars in Massachusetts were lined up with their lights flashing.

The suspects were separated from each other and given a ride to MDC headquarters, one to a car to foil the last chance to get their stories straight. This really wasn't necessary because the alcohol befuddled brains hadn't really come up with anything plausible in the hour before the cops arrived as they stood around kicking dirt.

When the caravan arrived at headquarters it was soon determined that there were no facilities to lock up the fifteen or so drunks so everyone was initially charged with trespassing, while the fuzz tried to come up with some other charges, and released on their own recognizance. They were also ordered to get the two planes off of the island, post haste.

Nate's 170 was no problem. He got a boat ride out the next morning and flew it back to the airport. PI's 180 was another matter, but the guys' were creative. They rounded up a few rowboats, some fifty-five gallon drums and a toolbox and towed the drums out to the scene of the crash. They had a few beers of course, as they took the wings off of the 180 (not as hard as it seems), strapped them to the floating drums and rowed them back to shore, ditto the fuselage.

There must have been some fuel and oil spillage during the process but it was 1969 and nobody gave a shit about things like that in those days.

There was a trial. Think *Alice's Restaurant.*

A high priced Boston lawyer who was a jumper and drinking buddy shredded the local prosecutors and got everyone off with a twenty dollar fine and the usual warnings. I think they suspended their fishing licenses for a year too, but nobody fished anyway.

Of course the U.S. Parachute Association got wind of the affair from some rat and grounded all participants for thirty days but as you'll recall from my night jump into The Inn episode we never paid any attention to that.

And then there was Jacques. Half of the people involved in the Quabbin disaster were PI employees. Nate was the Center manager, airport manager, chief pilot, instructor, mechanic and parachute rigger. Ed the pilot, Skip the pilot, Frank, instructor/ jumpmaster and three or four other jumpmasters. Terminated with prejudice! Banished from Orange and PI for life.

Jacques had good reason to be pissed off. Between the bad press, the trial, and the little matter of the $40,000 180 which was a smoking pile of scrap metal, most people would have done the same thing.

Firing everyone wasn't the end of Orange. My friend Bill took over and successfully ran the Center until 1979 but without Nate and a lot of the key people things would never be the same.

Chapter 16

Smoke and Flesh

At the time of the Quabbin Disaster I had already left P.I. and worked for a film company for a couple of years. We made the lowest of the low budget exploitation films called nudie movies; ie, soft-core porn. As I believe I mentioned before, this period is another book, but I want to tell you about another related event that occurred before I got back into the skydiving business.

How the film company went out of business is a long story so I'll cut to the chase. I was unemployed, along with Joe the cameraman, and Fitz, a film editor. (I was a soundman and editor). Fitz and I shared an apartment on West 52nd street in New York and Joe lived in an old frame house in a residential neighborhood in Bloomfield, just across the Hudson in New Jersey.

None of us had any money and it wasn't long until we were getting desperate enough to actually get a straight job, but after a bit of reflection and a few beers we had a meeting and decided to make our own movie.

Even in our optimistic altered mental state we realized that there were some obstacles that we had to overcome. We had no camera, sound equipment, lights, editing equipment, script, or place to shoot and edit the film. And, of course, no money.

To make an exploitation film that was marketable it had to be shot in 35 mm and be at least ninety minutes long. It could be black and white, as most were then. There were quite a few theaters in New York and around the country that screened these films for their mostly degenerate clients who were frequently jacking off in the balcony.

Joe had some contacts with producers for whom he'd done camera work so we got to work on a script and had it finished in a week. The movie's title was *Smoke and Flesh* and it centered around a party that's invaded by a group of Hell's Angels and the efforts of the partygoers to prevent the gang from raping and pillaging. It wasn't *Gone With The Wind* but the audience would be there to see tits and ass and we knew how to do that.

Joe found a backer with a name like Vinnie the Horse who agreed to put up $12,000 for us to deliver a finished film. We figured that we could shoot it for about $8000 if we were careful, and lucky, giving us enough to live on for six months (remember this was 1968).

Joe's house would be the interior location, because it was free, and we'd shoot the exteriors on the streets of Manhattan and Brooklyn.

Though filming permits are required for shooting in the streets we'd done it a hundred times without while working for the other company and were pretty good at bullshitting our way out of cop situations. Sometimes delivering a small bribe worked.

Joe started rounding up equipment from rental companies while Fitz and I made a list of the props we needed and lined up actors and actresses (hookers) who we'd worked with at the other company. We were paying $50 a day and they all bitched but signed on because in New York out of work actors and hookers are a dime a dozen and we had them by the balls. They also liked us.

Neither Fitz or I had a car so we took Joe's old station wagon and drove to a junkyard in Secaucus and bought a refrigerator for

$7. Of course after paying for it we figured out that it wouldn't fit in the wagon (duh), so we tied it to the roof with a piece of rope that the asshole junk guy charged us a dollar for. We dropped it off at Joe's place in Bloomfield and continued on our mission.

Next stop was a tobacco store for rolling papers and a pound of Prince Albert tobacco, a toy store where we bought a slot car racing game, and a pet store for a fifty gallon aquarium. This took a big bite out of the budget but we had written this great sex scene that featured a couple screwing on a bed shot through the aquarium with kissing Gourmais in the foreground. We agreed that it was worth the expense.

It was still two days until we started shooting so we decided to come back and get the fish after we got the aquarium up and running. Mistake!

The rest of the time before we started shooting was spent working on the house; blacking out the windows because the party scene took place at night, moving all Joe's stuff upstairs, and re-arranging the furniture so we could do dolly shots with the camera.

We set up the slot racing track and played with it for a while, cut a hole in the back of the refrigerator, and got the aquarium set up in the bedroom.

When Joe showed up with the equipment we set everything up and ran camera and sound checks until midnight and decided we were ready for lights, camera, action the next day. Except for the fish.

At six a.m. Fitz and I had a beer and headed off to the fish store leaving Joe to start rehearsing the actors when they showed up. We had to wait an hour for the store to open and it was 20 degrees out. We were freezing our ass off as we waited in Joe's car with no heater.

Our budget for the fish was about twenty bucks but they ended up costing 60 which really pissed us off but we decided we had no choice so the guy bagged them up and we fired up the Buick and headed back to Joe's, 40 minutes away.

There wasn't anywhere to park when we got there and we ended up lugging the bags of fish a block and a half to the house and threaded our way through the cast who were milling about as Joe explained the first scene.

Upstairs a big busted blonde named Susan lounged on the bed behind the aquarium in half bra and black lace panties smoking and reading the National Enquirer. She was supposed to be studying her lines but it's not too hard to remember how to moan.

We opened the bags and dumped the Gourmais into the aquarium, saw that they were swimming, and returned to the set and got the lights and sound set up for the first scene.

We did a couple of takes before Susan wandered downstairs and announced that the "fishies" didn't look too good. Fitz and I looked at each other and raced by Susan and up to the bedroom.

The "fishies" didn't just not look good, they were all floating on their backs. The water in the bags had probably dropped to almost freezing on the trip back from the fish store and we had dumped them into seventy degree water. Shocking!

I started swishing them around and told Fitz to get some salt. Somewhere in the dark recesses of my memory was something about salt reviving fish but I wasn't optimistic and I knew Joe was going to be pissed.

When Fitz got back I continued swishing the bodies around as he sprinkled pinches of salt on the surface. I really felt stupid stirring dead fish and praying for a miracle but after a few minutes gills started to quiver, tails wagged a bit and several of the Gourmais were actually swimming. Unfortunately half of them were terminal city and despite fifteen minutes of intensive care we flushed them. We still had three pair out of twelve original fish but didn't know how many were males or females. The scene depended on the fish kissing in front of the camera. If they were all one sex I was hoping they were gay.

We went back down and gave Joe the good/bad news as he was fastening the camera to the hole in the back of the refrigerator. We thought this was a great idea. The people at the party spike the bikers' beer with acid. One of the punks goes to get a beer from the fridge and the shot starts out black (inside the dark fridge) the door opens and the light comes on, the punk sticks his head in and reaches for a beer as Joe zooms in and out of focus to show the acid starting to work, door closes and the light goes out. It looked great on the big screen.

Fitz and I dumped the can of Prince Albert on the dining room table and started rolling tobacco joints for the main party scene while Joe set the camera up on the floor by the slot racing game and started shooting close ups of a tripping biker's face as he lay on the floor with the cars racing by him. The doorbell rang.

Joe opened the door and was face to face with two Bloomfield cops. I don't know why the neighbors would have called them just because a house in a residential neighborhood suddenly had the windows blacked out and a bunch of hookers going in and out but some people are just nosey.

Joe invited them in and the scene that greeted them included a gang of leather clad bikers, a half dozen bleached blondes in various states of undress, and a pound of what was apparently pot on the dining room table surrounded by rolling papers and rolled joints. Joe had to do a lot of talking but he was smooth and after about fifteen minutes of looking around and smelling the Prince Albert the cops left, telling us to keep the noise down

Two things saved our ass. They could see that we were shooting a movie and they didn't try to go upstairs where the cigarettes the girls were passing around weren't Prince Albert.

We finished the movie without incident, did the editing, and had a final print for Vinnie the Horse before he came looking for us.

We went to the opening in New York at a sleazy theater next to the West Side Highway. The bums actually clapped and cheered when our opening scene, a macro shot of fingers rolling a joint, filled the 40 foot screen in front of the title.

Chapter 17

John

I worked in the film business in New York for a while after Smoke and Flesh, acquired a wife and son, and worked at another parachute Center in New Jersey before opening my own place, Skydive East.

Because this book is about characters I've known and situations that I've been involved in I'm going forward to the 1980s' to recount some things that happened after my days at Orange and Lakewood.

In my dream at the beginning of this book I mentioned Greg (Mr. Sandwich), and his twin brother John, the pilot. They both worked at Skydive East and John saved my life, which he frequently reminded me of when he'd need a loan to tide him over until payday, or in Atlantic City when he and Greg were getting their ass whipped at the crap tables.

I gave John his first flying job when he was 18. I was running this place in South Jersey and a pilot had just quit, not unusual in our business. Young guys would fly jumpers for not much money to build up flying time and move on to commuter airlines or corporate flying when they had the qualifications.

Someone told me about John, who was pumping gas at a nearby airport. I really wasn't too interested in hiring someone that young to fly jumpers but I called him and told him to come in for an interview the next day.

He showed up in a suit and tie, which was pretty funny to a bunch of jumpers in shorts and t-shirts. He was skinny with blonde hair that had been hastily trimmed for the occasion and pretty nervous about applying for his first flying job.

I checked his logbook and he had a couple of hundred hours which was about the minimum needed to do the job. Our main airplane was a Cessna 205 that carried five jumpers and most of his flying time was in smaller Cessnas' but he was pretty confident and told me he'd been flying since he was fourteen, starting in gliders in England where his father worked at the time.

He'd gotten his pilot's license as soon as he turned sixteen and had been working low level jobs around airports in exchange for flying time to build up hours. He was excited about the chance to fly a bigger airplane and get enough time to make it to the airlines, his ultimate goal. I liked him and decided to give him a shot.

I had another jump pilot come in and fly with him for a few hours to make sure he could handle the plane and show him the procedures for flying jumpers and he did well so he was hired.

We had a couple of days of bad weather before we got a break in the clouds on a Friday afternoon. I checked weather and more storms were forecast but it looked like we had time to take that day's first jump course up before it got crappy again so I told John to pre-flight the plane and I got the students into their gear. There were eight of them so we'd have two flights, four students and me on each flight.

We boarded the 205 and took off, climbed to 2500 feet and I threw the wind streamer to pick the exit point as John circled back to start the first jump run.

I moved the first student to the edge of the open door, hooked up his static line, and was giving him last minute instructions when John tapped me on the shoulder and pointed toward the west.

The gray sky of a few minutes ago had turned blue black. I stuck my head out of the door and saw the ground crew rolling up the target (the signal to cancel the jump) and clouds of wind driven dust rising from the plowed fields surrounding the airport.

John nosed the plane over and reduced power as I got the students back into their seatbelts and stowed a few loose objects in preparation for landing. This was not a good situation. Jump pilots almost never land with a plane full of people. It's much harder than landing empty, as they would normally do, and John had never done it.

The storm front winds started to batter us as we came into the pattern, and John was 18. Bummer!

There are no seats in a jump plane except the pilot's, and I was strapped in on the floor next to John, my back to the instrument panel. He started a long final approach, battling the violent up and downdrafts and working the throttle in and out to maintain airspeed. The windsock on the end of the runway was showing a 90 degree crosswind and was in danger of ripping off of its pole.

We crossed the runway threshold at 100 feet above the ground and John banked the plane into the wind to stay lined up, planted the left wheel on the macadam, and struggled to keep control until we'd lost enough airspeed. He got the other wheel on the ground and braked to a stop with room to spare. "Not bad for a kid," I yelled at him over the engine noise as we taxied back to the hangar.

The flight office had recorded crosswinds of over 40 mph as we landed and everyone on the airport was impressed with the landing. John was going to fly for me for a long time but we'd always remember his first jump flight and that wasn't the only time he saved my life.

Chapter 18

Jim McGowan

I opened Skydive East at a small airport in western New Jersey in 1980.

Two partners and I scraped together a few thousand dollars and bought some used round parachutes, boots, coveralls and the parachute rigging equipment we needed to start a jump school.

We leased a sixty-foot trailer to serve as an office, classroom and post jump social club and after about a month of manual labor had a pretty nice setup and opened for business. One of my partners, Tom, was a pilot and owned a Cessna 182 jump plane that he contributed to the operation.

I was living in a small town an hour south of the airport with my wife and son and soon discovered that after working twelve or fourteen hours a day it was sometimes impossible to drive the two hours round trip and be back at work at seven in the morning.

Tom also needed a place to stay near the parachute Center so we, along with our office manager, Rosemary, rented a house a couple of miles from the airport. For no good reason that I can remember we dubbed the place the Snake Ranch, and that's where I first met Jim McGowan.

In the course of my skydiving career I've been interviewed hundreds of times by TV and newspaper reporters doing stories on skydiving. One question that invariably comes up is, having made thousands of jumps, which one do you remember the most. My answer is always, Jim McGowan.

The story starts in the late summer of our first year. A kid who worked for me named Skip told me about someone his mother worked with who wanted to skydive. Skip was about sixteen at the time and had worked for me since he was fourteen at another parachute Center. His mother was a technician at a blood lab in Philadelphia and her co-worker's name was Jim McGowan.

So far, so good. The guy wanted to jump. He had the $35 that the first jump course cost in those days, no problem. Problem! Skip then volunteered the information that McGowan was a paraplegic, paralyzed from the mid-chest down.

He'd called around to other parachuting Centers and they had all turned him down. No surprise there. Obviously one of the main elements of a parachute jump is landing on the ground and with the round parachutes that we used for students in those days the landings were pretty hard and it wasn't uncommon to have sprained ankles and an occasional fracture on the drop zone. Without the use of your legs it was guaranteed to be broken back city.

I told Skip to have Jim give me a call and I'd explain why he couldn't do it and thought that was the end of the matter and forgot about it.

A week or so later I was working in the office when McGowan called. He was 49 years old and had been confined to a wheelchair since he was 17 after being stabbed with a sword in a gang fight in a rough neighborhood in Brooklyn. He was pleasant on the phone but insisted that he wanted to jump. I explained why it wasn't possible but he talked me into meeting with him and I agreed, thinking that I could make my point better in person, and he sounded like someone that I'd like to know.

We met a week later at the Snake Ranch. Jim pulled up by himself in a beat-up Dodge rigged up with hand controls, his wheelchair stuffed into the back seat. I was a little surprised to see that this Irish McGowan that I was expecting was black.

Not being familiar with handicapped protocol I introduced myself and started to get his chair out of the back but he waved me off and reached over the seat and slid the chair out, flipped it open, and wheeled into the house.

A few of my staff and housemates were sitting around drinking beer, and Jim, a wide smile on his face, introduced himself and demanded some vodka.

We made small talk for a while and had supper before we got to the subject that I had been kind of avoiding, why he was going to be a more damaged paraplegic if he jumped out of an airplane. And I would be responsible.

We had a few more drinks and Jim gave his pitch. He'd done a lot of things since he'd been disabled. He played wheelchair sports, lived by himself, and held a full time job, commuting back and forth from the suburbs to the city everyday. He had always dreamed of flying and skydiving and was sure that there must be a way and we were his last hope.

My jumpmasters started throwing around ideas. "What if we caught him in a blanket?" What if he missed? "How about a net or an airbag?" All too risky, I thought. It would just take a wind shift to have him miss.

A dim light came on in my brain. Water? No one that I had ever heard of had made their first jump into water, but why not? With a lake big enough to assure that he wouldn't miss, it might work.

I tossed the idea out and a broad smile broke out on Jim's face while my other jumpmasters shook their heads. "I don't think it's legal."

"Fuck legal," I told them." Once the parachute gets wet it'll sink and drag him down." Someone said. "I'll give him water training to show him how to get out of his gear and we'll have divers in the water to help if he has trouble." I was cooking now. This was going to work.

We bullshitted for another hour before the tipsy, black paraplegic headed home and we sent somebody on a beer run and refined our plan.

The meeting at our house took place in September and it was a busy time of year at Skydive East. We had a lot of first jumpers and were working twelve-hour days and partying half the night but I spent rainy days and Tuesdays, our day off, to work on Jim's jump. He was calling me every other day and I admired his enthusiasm but he was driving me crazy. He wanted to jump tomorrow.

Some of the things that had to be arranged were: the water training for Jim, a place to make the jump, getting divers, communications systems, and last but by far not least, getting permission from the New Jersey Division of Aeronautics, who controlled our license, to allow a paraplegic to make his first jump into a lake.

I decided to get the lake lined up first and fortunately had a great spot that was only a few miles from the drop zone called Round Valley reservoir. I often fished there and it was about two miles in diameter and 200 feet deep in places. Even in the worst case scenario I figured he couldn't miss and I hoped that the depth didn't matter. If it became a factor it would be game over.

I knew one of the rangers that worked there and he steered me to his boss and I gave him my pitch, highlighting the great publicity that they'd get and avoided the probability that he'd be fired or get demoted to picking up dead deer carcasses from the highway in January if things went south. I was surprised that he agreed, with the condition that I get permission from the aviation authorities.

I called a scuba diver friend who put me in touch with his dive club in Princeton and got them on board, located ground to air radios that we could borrow, and just needed a pool to train Jim and get Aviation's permission. Jim, being psychic he claimed, called the next day and said that he'd gotten the use of the pool at Temple University, his alma mater, for a couple of hours a week. I now had to go to Trenton.

I had good relations with the Division of Aeronautics. The guys in Trenton all knew me from years of managing parachuting operations in New Jersey and, being pilots, thought that jumping out of airplanes was stupid and laid the same lame jokes on me every time I went down to their office for something.

I showed up on a Tuesday morning in my best preppy slacks and Izod sweater, fresh haircut and a dusty briefcase that I dug out of the back of my closet for a prop. After a short wait I was ushered into see Bert, the Chief Inspector.

Before he could start with the jokes I laid out the request and showed him the letter of permission from Round Valley and stressed the safety precautions that we would take and what great publicity this would be for the state.

He didn't say no, but said he'd have to check the regulations and talk to the other inspectors and would get back to me. I thought his response was fairly positive and drove home feeling optimistic that we were on our way.

That afternoon Jim called to see how the meeting went and I filled him in. He also had good news. A national TV show called *Evening Magazine* had contacted him and wanted to do a story on the jump. The stars were aligning.

Jim and I did two sessions in the pool at Temple and I taught him how to avoid getting wrapped up in the parachute after he hit the water, get rid of his reserve, and get out of his harness. I stressed that he had to be clear of the gear in about three minutes after which the wet canopy would become a five hundred pound anchor and take him to Davey Jones's locker.

It wasn't easy for Jim. Number one, he could barely swim, a fact I didn't learn until we first got into the pool. Try to swim sometime without using your legs. Number two, his hands were arthritic and he had a lot of trouble getting the canopy and harness releases open in the water. I had to pull him out a number of times before he mastered the technique but he finally got it.

Evening Magazine filmed the sessions at the pool and they did interviews with us as we trained and with Jim in his apartment. He was great on camera, really charming, a good speaker and always had a big smile on his face, even when they asked him, "Do you realize that you could die doing this?"

It was now mid-October and we were running out of time to get the jump off before the water in the reservoir would be too cold to do it safely. Though I had called Aeronautics several times I still didn't have an answer and tried again.

Bert got on the line and hemmed and hawed for a minute before he gave me the bad news. No dice. The regulations prohibited anyone who had less than fifty jumps from making a water jump. I pleaded my case for a couple of minutes but he was a bureaucrat and his boss, the Transportation Director, decided that Aeronautics would be sticking their neck out if something went wrong. They weren't going to change their mind. I felt sick when I hung up.

I tried to think of a way out before I called Jim. We could just go ahead and make the jump without the State's permission but they controlled the parachute Center license and could shut us down if we did it and Round Valley wouldn't let us jump without Aviation's okay. I called Jim.

I thought he would be devastated but he shook it off and full of his usual optimism said he'd make some phone calls. That didn't make me feel any better because he didn't have any connections that could help, or so I thought.

Depression set in and I lay awake every night trying to think of a way around the problem. Cold weather had arrived and business dropped off making things worse, and my employees, aware of my mood, were staying out of my way.

Jim and I hadn't spoken in more than a week and when he finally called he sounded exuberant. The people from *Evening*

Magazine, having some time and money invested in the story, had an idea. They had done a piece at a resort in the Pocono Mountains called White Beauty View Resort, the White Beauty being Lake Wallenpaupack, one of the largest lakes in Pennsylvania. Pennsylvania! No Division of Aeronautics, no Bert, no regulations. Why didn't I think of that?

Even better, Jim told me, the resort would give us free rooms and food for our crew and let the divers use their boats in return for the publicity. I hung up and broke open a bottle of JD.

It was nearing the end of October and the water temperature in the lake was already in the fifty's so Jim's jump was going to have to be put off until spring. This was tough for both of us but we stayed in contact and finally set the date for the 12th of May.

About a week before the jump date I went up to the resort, met the owners, and looked things over. The place consisted of a grand old hotel on the lake with about fifty guest rooms, several conference rooms, and a large central lobby with walk-in fireplaces and comfortable couch and chair arrangements scattered around. Picture windows provided a spectacular view of the lake and marina below and a formal restaurant adjoined the lobby, also with a great view of the lake.

The rejection by the New Jersey authorities had really turned out to be in our favor. If we had made the jump at Round Valley, which would have worked, there were only a few dumpy motels nearby and a Bagelsmith. This place was classy and free.

There was a nearby airport, Cherry Ridge, and I stopped in to see if the runway was long enough for us to take off in the jump plane Not only was it okay but they had a Cessna 207 with a cargo door that could be removed to make it a lot easier for Jim to jump. When I explained what we were doing they were glad to let us use it. Everything had fallen into place and now we just had to do it.

The week leading up to the jump, which was scheduled for the following Tuesday, was frantic. I was coordinating the divers, getting the equipment packed, and lining up transportation. I called the Associated Press and sent them a press release. They put out a story and our phones started ringing. Newspapers and TV stations from all over the New York and Philadelphia area were sending reporters and camera crews, including three news choppers. *Evening Magazine* was sending two camera crews and another helicopter.

During the week and weekend we were also running the parachute Center and adhering to our depraved after hours social schedule. By Monday afternoon we were exhausted but we loaded the gear, picked Jim up, and headed north to the Pocono's, arriving around sundown.

There were about ten of us from Skydive East, and Jim. We looked pretty grubby, after working at the Center all day, as we made our way through the lobby to our rooms, dragging our duffle bags and parachutes behind us.

Some reporters had already arrived but we fended them off until we got settled and cleaned up. We also set up our bar in one of the rooms and when we were primed enough went back to the lobby and gave a hell of a press conference. Jim was perfect, full of confidence with his winning smile, throwing out great sound bites. The media ate it up.

We finally broke away and got some supper and got back to our rooms around ten and had a few more drinks while we checked our gear and briefed the divers who had just arrived. I called the pilot and checked weather. Bad news, of course. The forecast was for rain starting in the early morning and lasting all day. The jump was scheduled for 10 o'clock and we could jump in the rain but the cloud ceiling was predicted to be much lower than the 3000 feet we needed to get the jump off.

As we all know, weather forecasts are often guesses and with all my time in the skydiving business I've learned to stick to the plan and hope they're wrong, which is how it turns out about fifty percent of the time.

A lot of the media people were staying at White Beauty and I knew where to find them so I went down to the bar and told them about the weather and suggested that they not fly the helicopters up until they checked with me in the morning. I crashed around one and McGowan and the rest of the crew were still partying.

The wind driven rain hitting my window woke me up before the alarm that I'd set for five went off. You know what I exclaimed!

The management of White Beauty had been very generous with their free room and food offer but we didn't want to seem greedy and had only asked for a couple of rooms for our crew and I looked around at disheveled bodies, including Jim's, scattered around the beds and in sleeping bags on the floor, all snoring and farting.

I called flight service. The forecast hadn't changed, the front was here and it was going to be crappy all day. Que Sera, Sera. We were here and we were going to throw this guy out of an airplane if it took a week.

The bodies gradually came to life as I spent the next hour on the phone; canceling the airplane, NOTAM with the FAA, the *Evening Magazine* crew, and then got some breakfast. I was actually in a pretty good mood, which surprised everybody who knew me.

We held a mini press conference in the lobby at ten o'clock and some of the reporters had to leave but promised to be back the next day. The rain pounded down on the lake as the divers and my jump crew bonded and wandered off to drink beer, sleep, and lay their best pick-up lines on the hotel maids, with some success according to them but you know how guys lie about that stuff.

Though I was quite confident that the jump was going to be successful there were still a lot of things that could go wrong. We weren't going to be able to practice Jim's exit from the plane until we got to the airport the next morning to see if he could move himself to the open door, hang his legs out in the ninety mile an hour slipstream, and launch himself out. I'd be beside him but couldn't do much to help move his 180 pounds, plus parachutes, around from my kneeling position in the plane.

His main parachute was static line deployed so he didn't have to pull a ripcord but it was critical that he launch himself into a stable fall position during the 3 or 4 seconds it took the canopy to open. If he tumbled on the exit he could get caught in the deploying lines and cause a malfunction.

The landing was also dicey. Jim would be wearing a radio receiver and my partner, Bill, would be helping him steer the parachute from a boat in the lake. On the way down Jim had to release one side of his front mounted reserve so he could quickly get out of his harness once in the water. If there was any wind the parachute canopy was likely to re-inflate after he landed and start dragging him setting up a dangerous situation.

The divers had assured me that they could get to Jim in a minute or two but they weren't taking into account the fact that he could have steering problems or the wind could pick up and he might be a couple of hundred yards from them.

Another item in my anxiety closet was the fact that what I thought was going to be a jump witnessed by the crew and a few friends was turning into a national media event and if things got screwed up I could picture myself on the cover of *Time* as the asshole of the year. I didn't sleep much Tuesday night.

It was foggy the next morning, with low clouds, but Flight Service gave me an optimistic forecast; clearing in the next couple of hours with winds of around 10 miles an hour. I told my crew and the divers to load the vans and check their equipment then re-filed a NOTAM with the FAA, called the airport and told them that the jump was on. They said that the plane was fueled and standing by.

I dragged Jim away from a gaggle of reporters and photographers in the lobby and we headed for Cherry Ridge, about seven miles away. The fog was lifting and the sun was breaking through the clouds. We were getting pumped.

The film crew was waiting for us and filmed as we lifted Jim and his wheelchair from the van and unloaded the parachutes and dive gear. Jim and I were going to be wearing wet suits and I changed into mine in the airport office bathroom as the divers stripped Jim in his wheelchair and wrestled him into his suit which was a laborious task. Making it more difficult was the fact that the suit that they'd brought was about two sizes too small and they had to shoehorn him into it. He looked like a sausage.

We had an hour until take-off but Jim and I got into our parachutes and went to the plane to practice the exit. All of the seats in the seven-place Cessna had been removed except the pilot's, as well as the cargo door, which left most of the right side of the plane open. We hoisted Jim into the plane and positioned him where he would be on take-off and then had him use his arms to scoot himself back to the open door and hang his legs out as he would on the jump. It was difficult for him but we went through it several times until I was confident that we could pull it off at 3000 feet. The cameras had been rolling since we'd gotten to the airport, except when Jim was naked in his wheelchair trying to get into his wet suit (Playgirl magazine didn't show up) and I could tell by the look on the reporter's faces that they couldn't believe this was happening. I could.

Fifteen minutes before takeoff I thought of something that I had overlooked. Jim had no control of his lower body and when he exited the plane and tried to stabilize himself in freefall his legs were going to be flopping around. I dove into my gear bag a found a thick, nylon parachute bridle cord and tied his legs together as he sat on the doorframe of the plane. I asked him if was too tight and hurting and he gave me a Duh! look. "I can't feel anything. I'm a paraplegic, dummy."

A cameraman and sound guy were going up with us and I helped them into parachutes and stressed that they stay away from the open door after Jim and I jumped unless they wanted to lose twenty grand worth of equipment and maybe their lives. They didn't need much convincing.

After I had them strapped in, Jim and I got in and the pilot fired up the engine to taxi to the end of the runway for take-off. I gave the pilot a thumbs-up and we roared down the runway.

As the plane broke ground I saw the cameraman panning his camera from Jim's empty wheelchair on the ramp to our plane as we started to climb. That was going to be a money shot!

When we were over the lake I could see the rescue boats with Bill and the divers spreading a blue tarp on the water, the target that Jim was to aim for. I could tell by the treetops below that the wind was picking up and I called Bill on the ground-to-air radio.

He told me his meter was reading 10 to 12 but there were higher gusts once in a while. Still okay but he'd watch it and call me if it changed.

We reached 3000 feet and started a wind streamer pass to determine how far upwind of the target Jim should exit. When I stuck my head out to throw the streamer it looked like the annual fly-in at Oshkosh; four helicopters tailing us and several small planes circling below. There was also a fleet of boats heading out of the marina to the target area. I leaned over to Jim and told him about the big audience and that he'd better not fuck up but they beeped that out of the show.

The exit point was a few hundred yards upwind of the target, not bad. I signaled the pilot to circle and start the jump run and helped Jim slide up to the door. As we approached the exit point I had started to get Jim's legs out when Bill called and told me the winds had picked up and to abort jump run. I motioned Jim back away from the door and called Bill back. He told me the winds were over fifteen and getting stronger, definitely too risky. Jim was protesting that he wanted to jump anyway.

We decided to orbit and wait. With three hours of fuel on the plane we could afford to fly around for a while and hope for a miracle but things were looking grim. High pressure had started to move in and I knew that usually meant wind.

Fifteen minutes later the situation hadn't changed so I told the boat crew and divers to go back to shore and keep an eye on the winds and we'd stay up until we were out of gas. We were getting cold and to make matters worse the zipper on Jim's tight wetsuit had split when he was moving around and was open from his neck to his crotch. We flew in circles for another hour.

On the lake below, the crew, reporters, and spectators had piled into the restaurant and ordered breakfast while Bill waited on the dock and monitored the wind meter. The wind finally started to drop and he called and said they were going back out on the lake and see how it looked. I didn't tell Jim because I didn't want to get him pumped up again in case we had to cancel.

When they were at the target area Bill called back. The winds were 10 to 15 but nothing higher. A little risky but worth a try and I told him we were going to give it another shot and started another jump run. Jim struggled to the door and got his legs out. I steadied him as he planted his hands on the door-frame and he turned to the camera, yelling over the roar of the engine.

"This is it. This is the moment that we've been waiting for."

I released my grip on his harness and got close to his ear, "Go for it, Jim."

The first paraplegic skydiver launched himself into space with his powerful arms and went into a pretty damn good arch and spread. Four seconds later he was hanging under the ugly green parachute, drifting towards the target. I was going to jump too but I had the plane circle until Jim was a few hundred feet above the target and I could see that the divers were going to be able to get to him quickly and I wouldn't have to help, then dove out and did a back loop for the camera.

I saw Jim being pulled aboard a pontoon boat and splashed down about ten feet away. After I crawled aboard I gave Jim a hug and a kiss and not all of the water running down our faces was water. It was just about the best moment of our lives.

Somebody opened a bottle of Champagne and Jim and I finished most of it before we got back to the dock.

We went to our rooms and got out of the wet suits and into dry clothes then met the mob of reporters and photographers in the hotel lobby and spent a couple of hours giving interviews and posing for pictures. We also kept drinking champagne.

The media finally left to write their stories and get the film back for the six o'clock news and Jim took a nap while I helped the crew dry out the parachutes and pack our gear up. It was after five o'clock by the time we were done and we gathered in one of the rooms with a couple of cases of beer and got tuned up for the big moment. We couldn't wait to see the jump on TV and at six turned on the tube and saw a picture of the Pope. He'd just been shot. The bastard! Why didn't he duck?

There went our coverage. The rest of the night all of the channels were all Pope all of the time. Bad Luck!

We did get some short TV pieces over the next couple of days and thanks to the AP, newspaper stories all over the country and the world, most featuring a great shot from a helicopter with Jim in the water right after he landed with his arms raised in jubilation.

Evening Magazine put together an excellent half hour show that ran on national TV a month or so later and Jim and I were swamped with calls from disabled people who wanted to jump. I had to explain that Jim's jump took months of work and I had a parachute Center to run. Now that we had proven that it could be done others would help them do the same thing, and many did.

Jim moved to Florida and continued jumping, eventually making twenty jumps including freefalls from 12,000 feet where he formed a star formation with 7 other jumpers in freefall. In 1984 we returned to Lake Wallenpaupack and attempted to have Jim hookup in freefall with another paraplegic on a freefall from 10,000 feet. The hookup wasn't successful but it was a great jump.

Jim and I became good friends and saw each other often over the next twenty years as he continued to jump, flew gliders, attempted to swim the English Channel and wrote four books.

He contracted a blood infection two years ago and died at 76 years old.

Chapter 19

Memorial Ditch Weekend

McGowan's jump was May 13th and we went back to our old routine at the parachute Center, training bunches of first jump students and tossing them out. At the end of almost every day we hung around the trailer/office, barbecued, drank and told war stories, swooped on the girls, and generally got stupid. The pilots and instructors were under intense pressure every day, entrusted with the lives of fledgling skydivers, and they and the rest of our staff deservedly let their hair down after the sun set and the planes were tied down. Which brings us to Memorial Ditch Weekend.

The main players were my partner in Skydive East, Dick, who I started skydiving with in 1960, John the pilot, Mindy, one of my jumpmasters, and Dr. Rick, one of the experienced jumpers at the Center.

It was Memorial Day weekend and by Monday night we had been going full tilt for three days and were ready to party. As soon as the last customers had been de-briefed, bought their T-shirts and headed back to the city, we fired up the barbecue and started working on the beer, hard stuff, and made occasional trips to the woods or cars for a smoke.

After three or four hours it started to rain and I had an opportunity to fall in love for the night and drove back to the Snake Ranch with my new friend hoping to get lucky. The hardcore players were still whooping it up.

My office manager/ housemother, Rose, showed up soon
after we got home and we started downing shots of JD and
were shooting the shit when the phone rang. It was Dick, and
it seems that he was stuck in a ditch. That turned out to be the
understatement of the century.

There was not the slightest possibility that any of the three of
us could drive in our condition and I told him to call a tow truck
and hung up.

The distance from the Center to the Snake Ranch is about 3
miles and the roads are two-lane country and always deserted
late at night. With Dick leading the way, he and John had closed
down the party at the center and headed for the house. John was on
Dick's ass and tapped his bumper several times as they raced down
the dark roads. I know this sounds stupid but we all had pretty
good reflexes, even when we were impaired and John and I had
played the same game when he was eighteen and first working for
me. There was no danger to others on the remote back roads and
we thought we were invincible.

About a mile away from the airport Dick came to a
T-intersection. Trying to shake off John he slowed just enough, he
thought, to run the stop sign and whip a turn, losing the pursuer.
He didn't account for the wet pavement and fish-tailed a couple of
times before plunging into a six-foot deep ditch, nose first, wedged
up against a telephone pole.

John skidded to a stop past the crash site and backed up onto
the edge of the road where his back wheels promptly sank to the
axels in the mud as the light rain turned into a downpour. He
ran across the road to check on Dick who had crawled out of his

passenger door and was standing genital deep in muddy water, screaming obscenities.

Dick finally calmed down and they came up with a plan. There was a nearby house where the owner of a sod farm lived and we'd had some dealings with him so Dick walked to the house to make the fruitless call to me while John hiked back to the airport and woke up Kent, the owner, and asked if he could borrow his tractor.

John, muddy, soaking wet and drunk, actually talked him into giving him the keys and a rope and drove the tractor back to the scene, hooked the rope to Dick's rear axel and started pulling. The car was halfway out and John was backing up at full throttle when the rope, rotten they now discovered, snapped and the tractor and John hurtled backwards into the opposite six foot ditch. When John climbed back up onto the road Dick observed that he was a stupid bastard for getting them into this, and Kent was a motherfucker for giving them a bad rope, and Doug was an asshole for not coming to get them, and on and on.

A set of headlights appeared, and though you would think that this was good news, anyone who came upon the scene (two cars and a tractor in ditches) was going to call the cops which meant that Dick and John were facing DWIs' and John could lose his pilots license. But they got lucky. It was Mindy, her head just showing above the steering wheel of her three ton Buick.

As I mentioned Mindy was a jumpmaster. In her early twenties, she was a really cute blonde, under five feet tall and weighing all of 90 pounds. She stopped and stared in amazement at the carnage before bursting into hysterical laughter (she was also drunk) and the two chauvinists told her to shut the fuck up and go to the Snake Ranch for help.

She got back in her car, still laughing, and got at least a hundred yards into her mission when she swerved off the road and became the fourth casualty, mired in the mud.

John and Dick sought refuge from the pouring rain in the Buick with Mindy and realized that they were really screwed. They were seriously out of options, even John, who was always able to come up with something in tight situations. Depression set in.

It was one a.m. when Doctor Rick showed up. He wasn't really a Doctor but that's what we called him. He'd gone to a local bar after the party at the airport and was on his way to the Snake Ranch to crash. He was drunk too but avoided the ditch.

Everyone piled in Rick's car and made it to the house. John got on the phone and found a 24 hour towing service. He told the guy that his car was kind of stuck in a ditch and gave him directions. The driver was reluctant to come out in the pouring rain at now one thirty but finally agreed and Rick drove John and Dick back to the scene.

The guy was enraged when he arrived and saw what he had to deal with but Rick and John, with some help from the roll of cash that Rick always carried, kept him from leaving.

They pulled the tractor out first and John drove it back to the airport while Rick and Dick helped the tow truck guy get the other three cars out. Mindy's and John's were drivable and the truck towed Dick's back to the garage to be retrieved the next day.

They picked John up at the airport and by three a.m. stumbled into the house; wet, cold, muddy, and sober. They were relieved to have escaped the law, and except for Dick's car, which was pretty beat up, there wasn't a lot of damage and no one got hurt. You would of thought that they'd learned a lesson. Fat chance!

I got up to take a piss around 10 in the morning and they were doing shots and beer.

Chapter 20

How John Saved My Life, Again

John built up enough hours flying jumpers to get jobs with small airlines flying commuters and eventually made the big time when he was hired by a major airline in the early '80's.

He continued to fly for me at Skydive East when he wasn't at his real job though his contract with the airline had a condition that he couldn't fly with anyone else for pay. We got around that by an under the table arrangement but he still had to be careful he wasn't caught.

On a busy day in August the Center was humming with fifty first jump students and we were using three airplanes. John was flying our Cessna 206, which carried a jumpmaster and five students.

I was training half the course and around three o'clock they were ready to go up and scare themselves to death. I assigned them to their flights and the flight line crew got them into their cumbersome main and reserve parachutes, helmets and goggles. We still used military T-10 parachutes because of their reliability but they were big, 35 feet in diameter, and an ugly army green. The combined weight of the main and reserve was about 40 pounds and of course the students all complained. The 200 pound macho guys complained the loudest and the 100 pound girls usually just dealt with it

When my first flight was ready I double checked their gear and gave them a few last minute reminders about what they were supposed to do and walked them out to the plane, steering them away from the propeller spinning a couple of thousand rpm's. It always baffled me how many of them would try to make mincemeat of themselves by walking straight towards it. But then in about ten minutes they'd be standing outside the plane at three thousand feet above the ground flying ninety miles an hour and then jump off. In their minds it was probably about the same thing.

I helped the students into the 206 and got them into their positions on the floor. After they had their seat belts on I knelt on the floor next to John and gave him the thumbs up to taxi.

We took off and climbed to twenty five hundred feet and dropped a wind streamer, determined the exit point, and I hooked up the first student's static line. He swung his feet out, John slowed the plane, and I gave him the get set command and helped him climb out on to the eighteen-inch jump step. I yelled "GO," two or three times and he executed a perfect back loop, unfortunately, as I had been teaching him how to leave in an arch and spread for the last four hours. His feet hit the deploying parachute lines but it opened as they almost always did despite our customer's best efforts to prevent it.

I pulled in the deployment bag, put the rest of the flight out and repeated the cycle for three more. We landed and taxied to pick up the last group, which turned out to be three big New York City cops. I could see the light at the end of the tunnel. One more flight, debrief the students, sell them some second jump tickets and T-shirts and it would be martini time.

The field where we dropped the students was about four miles from the airport. We took off with the last group, made a turn to head south to the drop zone and John started to climb to jump altitude. At five hundred feet I unfastened the student's seat belts and was organizing the manifest sheets on my clipboard when there was terrible bang that was like a mortar round exploding six feet in front of my face. Blue smoke started streaming up from under the rudder pedals and filling the cockpit. It took me a couple of seconds longer than John to realize that it was suddenly quiet, i.e., no engine. I looked at my altimeter and it read twelve hundred feet and dropping.

John yelled seat belts and started radioing back to the airport on our company frequency that we'd lost the engine and were going down. I scrambled to fasten the students seat belts, an awkward task when you're sitting on the ground but a nightmare in a plummeting aircraft with shaky hands, as John banked hard to the left and pushed the nose down looking for a field long and flat enough to get the plane down in one piece.

I got the last belt fastened and sat down with my back against the instrument panel as we passed through four hundred feet. John calmly told us to hang on, which I thought unnecessary, and braced myself for whatever was coming. I could see trees rushing by out of the side window.

As the plane touched the ground and bounced a few feet back into the air I flipped the handle on the jump door to the open position so that we wouldn't be trapped if we crashed and there was a fire. We hit the ground again and stayed down bumping violently on the uneven ground as John struggled to control the plane and stood on the brakes until we skidded to a stop.

Smoke was still filling the cockpit as we scrambled out and checked our underwear. I saw that we had stopped a few hundred feet short of a large ditch and patch of woods, that would have made the outcome much less favorable.

John had done it again. I'd be buying him drinks for the rest of his life, gladly.

The smoke had stopped and we looked around, trying to figure out where we were. It was a farm field with a shed in the middle but there were no houses in sight. We got out of our parachutes and were deciding whether to start walking or wait to be rescued when we were surrounded by dozens of elk who strolled out of the woods and an adjoining field to see what was going on.

We knew where we were. The farm was our previous drop zone, part of which was populated by elk. In the hectic two minutes after the engine explosion John only saw one place to land and it happened to be here.

We tried the radio but couldn't raise anybody and were getting ready to head out when an approaching helicopter scattered the elk and landed next to us in a cloud of dust. The two cops who climbed out had been patrolling the nearby Delaware River and heard John's Mayday call and stopped to see if we were okay.

They wanted to call the Aviation Authorities to report the emergency landing but John and I assured them that help was on the way and there was no need to bother anybody (and get John busted by the airline).

I hiked over to the owner's house and told him what happened and borrowed his phone to call the Center to get a van to pick us up.

When we got back I talked the cop/students into continuing their mission, put them in another plane, took them up, and dropped them on their first jump. Good for them. Though their friends back in the Big Apple would never believe their story I was impressed that they did it.

That was the second time John saved my life but I always reminded him that he had ulterior motives because his ass was in that airplane too.

Chapter 21

Night Over Water

Though the flights with John were dangerous they weren't the worst things that happened to me in airplanes. If you're the average person who jumps on a commercial flight once in a while to go visit grandma or throw some money away at the crap tables in Vegas, it's unlikely that you're going to run into trouble.

Jump planes and military aircraft are another story; the former because they're often older and not maintained to airline standards and the latter because of the missions that they perform like landing on carriers.

I've crawled out of a twin engine Beechcraft that ground looped at ninety mph on take off and ended up ten feet from the woods due to the inexperience of the pilot who had just purchased the plane and had a two-hour checkout.

Four feet of wing was torn off the A3D our crew was flying in a mid-air collision over the Atlantic when our wingman sneezed at 400 knots and bashed us (we made it back to the ship), had engine failures, stuck landing gear, electrical fires, hit by lightning over the Black Sea, etc. It's all part of that kind of flying, and the outcome, despite all of the best efforts of the crew, is often determined by only luck. Which brings me to the next story.

As I mentioned earlier, I made a number of Med cruises in the Navy. Our routine was to pack up all of our equipment and personal gear at our base in Sanford, Florida and fly our squadron's twelve Heavy Attack bombers to the navy base in Norfolk, Virginia to meet the carrier, which in this case was the USS Roosevelt.

We'd spend a couple of days there waiting for the ship to finish taking on supplies and getting our last taste of alcohol and sex before deploying. This was not a time for moderation as we weren't likely to encounter either until we had liberty in Europe a month to six weeks later.

The ship would set sail and when it was a hundred miles or so off shore our squadron, along with fighter, light attack, and sub hunting squadrons would fly out of Norfolk and land on the carrier and head for Europe.

The purpose of the Med cruise was to provide a military presence in the area and to train flight crews so we flew almost every day, or in my case, night. My pilot, Lonnie, was a Lt. Commander and most of the other pilots were higher ranking Commanders and Captains who took the day flights and gave us the night shift.

There were pros and cons to this. The mess areas weren't crowded at night and when we got back from our flights we could get a shower without standing in line. There were four thousand other bodies floating with us.

Landing on an aircraft carrier at night is challenging. We usually were simulating combat conditions and the ship had all lights above decks turned off except a couple of dim red center lights on the flight deck for the planes to line up on. We flew four hour simulated bombing missions to targets more than a thousand miles from the ship and had to return and find it, often in bad weather and low on fuel, and catch a wire on a pitching deck eight hundred feet long.

This incident occurred about a hundred miles off the coast of France. We'd returned from a practice radar bombing mission to

Marrakech, off the north coast of Africa, and entered the landing pattern with about a dozen other planes returning from their missions.

Though we launched with thirty thousand pounds of fuel, enough for four and a half hours of flight, we were now down to about five or six thousand, which was the maximum weight we could land on the ship with.

A couple of F-4's landed ahead of us and we were cleared for final and lined up with the deck, starting our approach. Lonnie pulled back the throttles and reduced our speed to 150 knots and we each locked our shoulder harness and braced ourselves for the violent deceleration when we caught the arresting wire.

My seat was facing aft, back-to-back with Lonnie, and I didn't see us slip below the glide path when we were a few hundred yards from touchdown. I heard the engine power increase and then sputter as we slammed into the deck and Lonnie jammed the throttles forward and the engines roared to life as we raced down the deck and were airborne again.

This is a normal occurrence called a bolter. When the aircraft wheels hit the deck the throttles are pushed forward to takeoff power. If you catch the wire you still stop, if you miss the wire you're starting to take off for another pass. There would be no time to accelerate enough to get off the eight hundred foot deck if you weren't already at full throttle.

Lonnie usually caught the wire on the first pass but sometime we'd miss so this was no big deal. The concern was the engine compressor stall on final, and we'd hit the deck pretty hard. We started another pattern behind some of the other planes landing and went over our check list again. I was hungry, had to piss, and was anxious to get down

Our next approach was right on the money, Lonnie planted the wheels in the middle of the four arresting wires and I braced for the G's but it didn't happen and we were airborne again. Lonnie asked flight control for a fly by the bridge so they could check our tail hook.

I swiveled around to look at the fuel gauge. Still thirty minutes, we were okay. The guys on the bridge said the tail hook looked okay and we went around for our third pass, and our fourth, and by our seventh we knew something was wrong. We were touching down right on the money and not getting hooked.

Then the ship called. A seaman apprentice had just found our tail hook lying on the deck. There's a tail bumper that hangs down near where the tail hook on the plane is located and the guys on the bridge had mistaken that for the hook six passes ago. Thanks, you assholes, we're going to run out of gas. My ninety dollars a month flight pay wasn't starting to look so good.

Bain, the navigator yanked out his flight charts and started looking for a place to land or crash softly on the coast of France while Lonnie used most of our remaining gas to climb to seven grand in case we had to bail out before we got to land.

I secured all the loose gear and checked my parachute and survival equipment. I wasn't looking forward to making my first jump from a crippled jet, over water, at night, and wished that I'd paid more attention to my survival classes rather than dozing off a hangover.

We spotted the lights on land about the same time the left engine sputtered to a stop. Lonnie switched fuel tanks and restarted the engine as Bain found the only airport on his chart within range, Istre, which had about half the runway length that we needed to land safely. He gave Lonnie a heading as the right engine quit.

Lonnie radioed Mayday to the ship and told Bain and I to get ready to bail out. I pulled the lever that blew the bottom hatch open and unfastened my seat belt and shoulder harness, looking at the black water rushing by a mile below. I would be the first one out, followed by Bain and Lonnie.

It was then that Bain yelled "lights." They had just blinked on a few miles away and it was a runway. It was Istre.

Lonnie pushed the nose over and nursed our crippled bomber toward the airport, burning off altitude and swinging wide for the approach as Bain and I belted ourselves in and unfastened our parachute harness and survival gear in preparation for a quick exit after we landed. Now I was scared!

The lone engine kept running until Lonnie planted the wheels on the first fifty feet of the runway, cut the power, and switched off the automatic braking system. He stood on the brakes and we skidded, tires smoking and screeching, to the end of the macadam and a few hundred feet beyond where one of the landing gear partially collapsed and brought us to a smoking stop.

We scrambled out of the hatch and looked for fire, but the smoke was just from the smoldering tires and brakes, glowing red in the darkness. My first order of business was to unzip my flight suit and take my long delayed piss, and considering the recent events, I was surprised that I'd lasted until we were down.

A beat up jeep roared up and a very excited Frenchman jumped out and surveyed the wreckage. He spoke enough English to tell us that he'd closed the airport for the night and was locking the office when he heard our Mayday call and turned the runway lights back on. Remember what I said about luck. In another five minutes we'd have been hanging in our parachutes ten miles off shore.

We contacted the carrier and told them to call off the search and our savior gave us a ride to the nearest town, Marseilles, where we crashed for the night.

When we looked at the plane in the morning we found that the rear area where the tail hook had been located had been smashed in by hitting the back edge of the carrier deck on our first landing attempt. Inside the tail compartment was about a bushel basket's worth of rivets that had popped out of the tail when we hit. The mechanics who were flown in from the Roosevelt a couple of days later told us that the tail should have fallen off on the flight to land.

Chapter 22

Naked

Jeff, Kenny, and Mike were a small posse of experienced jumpers who occasionally jumped and hung around Skydive East. They belonged to a skydiving club in Pennsylvania called The Herd that was notorious for their hardcore skydiving and harder core parties. The main event at their annual Herd Boogie, in addition to heavy duty drinking, recreational drug use, wet T-shirt contests, and free wheeling sex, was the burning of a guest's car (usually an aging clunker that could be replaced for a couple of hundred bucks). The Herd was a tough bunch.

Jeff and the guys weren't the baddest boys though, and were more into practical jokes than the destructive behavior of their peers, which made them welcome at our place.

They always showed up at the Midsummer Night's Ball and Jeff was the pyrotechnic guy, driving in with his trunk loaded with the finest M-80's, aerial bombs, and really professional fire works. As soon as it got dark he'd start shooting and keep going until the party ended or the cops showed up.

To pick up some extra income for jump money they also performed demonstration jumps for events like town celebrations, summer camps, and corporate parties. Jeff did the organizing; lining up the jumpers, getting the FAA clearances, reserving a plane, and dealing with the client.

One summer weekend at the Herd, Jeff announced that he had a jump scheduled for the following week. Mike and Ken were available so they needed one more jumper, but there was one more thing, the jump was into a nudist camp and they had to jump naked.

Now the Herd crowd was a tough bunch but there weren't many takers for the fourth slot on the jump. Most of the guys seemed to think that their equipment was not adequate for this kind of jump, if you know what I mean. You can't cross your legs when you're hanging in a parachute harness.

But there was a guy named Bob, who only had a hundred jumps and had never made a demonstration jump. He was game and Jeff agreed and told him to meet them at the airport on the appointed day.

Though Bob must have had second thoughts, and probably weird dreams in the interim, he arrived at the airport with his gear and joined the guys at the plane. It was a busy day at the airport and there were a lot of spectators roaming around with their kids, watching the planes take off and land, so the plan was to stay dressed until the plane was in the air and then change into their non-costumes.

Before they climbed aboard Jeff went over the plan. He told Bob that he was to climb out on the plane's step on jump run, jump first when Jeff gave the signal, and open at three thousand feet. The others would follow him out and open lower so Bob could follow them into the camp.

After taking off, Jeff gave the pilot a heading to fly to the jump site and started undressing. This was not a small feat with four jumpers and the pilot crammed into the cabin of the small Cessna. It required getting out of their parachutes, taking off their jump suits and underwear, then getting back into their parachute harnesses without damaging any sensitive body parts. Think of it as a game of aerial twister.

Bob was understandably nervous. He'd never been on a demonstration jump before, was naked, and didn't know where the nudist camp was. Poor Bob.

They stowed their jump suits and bvds under the pilot's seat so they wouldn't blow out of the plane when they opened the door on jump run and gave each other a gear check (I'm talking parachutes here) as they arrived at the jump site and circled for jump run.

Bob was desperately pressing his face against the window, trying to find the nudist camp, beads of sweat clinging to his forehead as Jeff opened the jump door and stuck his head out to spot.

The pilot slowed the plane and Jeff tapped Bob and pointed to the jump step. Bob struggled onto the step and looked back at Jeff who slapped him on the ass and screamed "GO." Bob stepped off and stabilized as he looked up for his teammates he saw Jeff's middle finger. The door of the plane closed, leaving him alone in freefall.

Panic set in as he looked down and did a slow turn, looking for the nudist camp, but all he could see below was a congested suburb of Allentown, and a giant mall.

His altimeter needle was approaching three thousand feet when he deployed his 'chute and he continued to look for the landing area, east and west, north and south, nothing that looked like a camp. That's because there wasn't a camp, or nudists, or a demonstration jump, except the one Bob was making as he descended with genitals flapping, into the middle of the crowded mall.

The descending parachute certainly got the crowd's attention and by the time Bob was down to five hundred feet he was visible enough to cause the spectators to cover their children's eyes or herd them inside the mall. And by the time he landed security was well on their way.

Poor Bob! At least he could now wrap the parachute around himself and try to slink off and find a ride back to the airport, which he eventually did. On the way he thought long and hard about what would be the most gruesome and painful way to kill Jeff. He probably still is.

Chapter 23

The Chase

Jealousy can be a very bad thing. It can threaten relationships, be the motivation for violence and murder. Even start wars. The wrong person in the throes of jealousy is capable of irrational and dangerous actions. Mark was such a person.

The following took place at Sky Manor Airport where Skydive East had its base of operations. By now we had moved from the trailer that we operated in during our first year of business into a hangar that we leased from the airport. We'd built a classroom and office in one end and used the rest to store the planes at night and as a packing area during the day. Student jumpers would register and pay for their jumps in the office, train in the classroom and outdoor training area, and when ready to jump, board a plane and fly to our drop area five miles away to make their jump.

We couldn't land jumpers on the airport due to the air traffic and a glider operation that operated off of a grass strip that paralleled the main runway. The jumpers and equipment were shuttled back and forth from the farm field that we used as a drop zone.

On this weekend we'd hired another airplane, in addition to our two Cessnas, a ten place DeHavilland Beaver, owned and flown by a friend of mine named Woody.

The Beaver was similar to the Noordyn Norsemen that we flew at P.I., and as the Norsemen were, used extensively in Alaska for flying in and out of remote areas.

Woody was in his early fifty's, grizzled looking, a beer gut, always unshaven and usually hung over. He was also a jumper and had logged a couple of thousand jumps, starting in the early days of the sport, as I had, and flew to different parachute Centers on weekends from his base in upstate New York. I had recently hired him for a filming segment for a soap opera. The director thought that he looked so much like a bush pilot that he fired the actor who was to play the pilot and used Woody instead.

It was late in the afternoon and things were humming along. A group of students' were going up for their jumps and coming back to get de-briefed. The experienced jumpers were having a good time jumping the Beaver when Harry, our ground instructor, called me on the CB from the drop zone announcing that there was trouble.

Someone was driving a white van with Pennsylvania plates around the landing field trying to run over people. And they thought that the guy had a gun. After Harry assured me that he wasn't fucking around with me I told him to get people into our vans and I called 911.

The cop wanted to know where I was and I had to explain that I was at the airport but the problem was five miles away and told them where. He still seemed confused but said that they'd be on the way.

I was now inclined to head to the drop zone but thought better of it. If the cops were on the way they would be there before I would be and I decided I'd be better off staying in the office where we had phones and radios. I called Harry back to get an update.

The bad guy, he said, was parked on the field now, and watching them. He'd found out that his name was Mark and he was the ex-boyfriend of a girl who worked for us, helping the students with their equipment and driving our vans. She told Harry that he did own a gun.

The cops, being cops, showed up at the airport a few minutes later, rather than the drop zone where the bad guy was. Using small words that I hoped they'd understand, I repeated that the guy causing the trouble wasn't at the airport and sent them on their way.

A few minutes passed and Harry called back and said that the guy had left the field and might be heading for the airport.

Though I'd given the boys in blue a description of the vehicle that they were looking for, they passed it about half way to the drop zone as the gunman headed for the airport. Not finding his paramour on the landing area he had headed for our office.

Harry, a 220 pound body builder and Army veteran was my main source of support in physical disputes that would arise from time to time but he was five miles away and we had students in the air. I looked around for Tony, an experienced jumper that I knew was jumping that day, and a good substitute for Harry. He wasn't a muscleman and was painfully soft spoken but he was a decorated ex-Navy Seal, an asset we needed in this situation

At this point I wrote off the fuzz. By the time they could figure things out it might be too late. Rosemary told me that Tony might be in the restaurant and I jogged over and found him working on a plate of greasy eggs.

His eyes lit up when I explained the situation. My plan was to keep an eye out for the intruder and if he did show up prevent him from causing trouble until the cops got there.

We were half way to the office when the white van pulled into the parking lot and stopped, facing our hangar. The occupant turned off the engine and sat staring through the tinted window as Tony and I returned to the office and decided what to do next.

Waiting for the cops was one option but if the guy got out of the van before they got there, with a gun, there was no telling what would happen next. There were a lot of people walking around the airport including families with kids and we decided to position ourselves to make a move on the guy if he tried to leave the van.

We left the office by a back door, circled around behind the vehicle and crouched behind another car a few feet away. A few minutes passed and still no gendarme. Tony decided we should move in and take him out. I wasn't thrilled with the idea but he convinced me that if we came up on both sides and yanked the doors open at the same time we could disable the guy before he could react. Tony volunteered to take the driver's side and I didn't argue.

We split up and worked our way closer, staying out of the range of the rearview mirrors. When we were within a few feet the engine roared to life and our target raced out of the parking lot and down the airport driveway toward Pittstown road.

Tony and I ran to the office and I grabbed a ground to air radio and called Woody in the Beaver as he entered the pattern after dropping a flight. He could see the van and said it was heading north and said he'd follow it and stay in touch.

I told Rosemary to give the cops one of our radios to monitor Woody's transmissions, if they ever showed up, and Tony and I jumped in a company van and raced after the culprit. Our adrenaline was flowing and we were consumed with righteous wrath. The bastard was escaping.

When we hit the main road and headed north I checked in with Woody. He had the target in sight a mile or two ahead of us. The Beaver was at five hundred feet and I could picture him morphing into Slim Pickens in *Dr. Strangelove.* This was his kind of stuff.

We blew through the great metropolis of Pittstown (population 1500) forty miles over the speed limit and at Woody's direction turned onto a winding dirt road that came to a dead end at the site of a house under construction. The white van was parked, empty, with the driver's door ajar. The quarry was gone.

The cops had been following the chase on the ground to air and they showed up a few minutes later. After a few minutes of blah, blah, blah they decided he was probably in the woods across an open field near us and started after him. They were perfect targets if the guy started shooting. The situation was now out of our hands and I called Woody and told him to go back to the airport before he ran out of gas and Tony and I drove back to the office.

It took three days for the authorities to locate the suspect (at another girlfriend's house) and because no one was hurt and they never found the gun he ended up getting some probation.

At least we had something to talk about for a while.

Chapter 24

Name Dropper

I'm sure you remember the movie Forest Gump. He's this slow-witted guy who stumbles into all of these historical situations and meets a bunch of famous people by chance. *Orange* is about people, and so far, though interesting, I hope, they haven't been famous. But I have had some Forest Gump experiences. This is one of them.

April 21st, 1990, started out as an average spring Sunday at Skydive East. The weather was nice but a front was forecast to move in that afternoon, bringing low clouds which might interfere with the first jumpers making their jumps. We had about thirty scheduled and I reminded the staff that we had to keep things moving to get as many jumpers out as possible before that happened.

The first jump course started at ten and after a one hour lecture the students had a lunch break and spent two or three hours in the outdoor training area practicing emergency procedures, aircraft exits, and parachute landing falls. They were then theoretically ready to jump. I say theoretically because even though they had to demonstrate all of the procedures to the instructor's satisfaction, the reality was that some of them were going to leave the aircraft back looping off of the step, kicking their feet, waving their arms, and an assortment of other aerial maneuvers instead of the stable fall position that we had practiced and drummed into their heads for the last four hours.

Despite their efforts to foil the parachute opening they would be hanging under the canopy in a state of shock until the ground instructor talked them into grabbing their steering toggles and attempted to steer them into the drop zone where many again experienced brain lock as the ground approached and dug holes in the farm field instead of performing a parachute landing fall..

I've trained and put out over twenty thousand first jumpers and to be fair, a lot of them have made perfect stable exits from the plane, steered their parachutes right to the target, and performed a perfect landing, even with a radio failure. Unfortunately they weren't in the majority.

By the time I'd briefed the staff, checked on the planes, and taken care of a few other things it was nine-thirty and the novices were handing over their hard earned money and filling out their registration forms and a three page waiver that told them at least three times that they faced possible death or serious injury by jumping out of an airplane and it wasn't our fault. Their mothers and friends had already told them that before they left home so it didn't scare them any more than they already were.

I straightened up the classroom (gotten rid of the empty beer cans from Saturday night) and checked over my teaching material as the first students wandered in and by ten most of the chairs were full except for the first row. I introduced myself and was a few minutes into the lecture when Tammy poked her head through the office door and asked if I could take four guys who had just arrived.

This was a regular occurrence and wasn't a problem, I could catch them up on what they'd missed at the end of the lecture, and it was another couple of hundred bucks. Come on down.

They came in the back door of the classroom and as they made their way down to the front row I guessed they were New York, business, in their late twenties, basically Yuppies. Nothing wrong with that, we had a lot of them. They had money, were for the most part polite and educated, and if they had fun they'd bring back their friends.

My staff tried hard to treat everyone the same. You could be a bum from skid row who'd found a hundred bucks in the gutter and decided he wanted to skydive before his liver gave out or a CEO with a mid-life crisis and nothing would be different. Same training, equipment, hand holding. Isn't this a great country!

The new guys apologized for the late arrival and I introduced myself again and as I continued with the lecture I thought that I'd seen one of them, more athletic looking than the others, before. His name tag said John. He might have been a sit thru; someone who'd jumped before and waited too long to come back, having to repeat the course. He really looked familiar.

When the lecture was over I gave the class a lunch break and filled in the late guys on what they'd missed. I told them to go out to the desk and fill out their paperwork, get some lunch, and I'd see them in the training area.

While I was straightening up the chairs one of the pilots came in looking for duct tape to fix something that was falling off of one of the planes, followed by Tammy, from the office, looking seriously excited. I was afraid to ask.

"What?"

"Do you know who's in the course?" she asked, breathlessly.

"One of the guys who came in late looks familiar."

"You dumb ass," she complimented me, "It's JFK, Jr."

Gulp. Pressure's on.

I'd dealt with my fair share of celebrities. Christy Brinkley and her boyfriend of the moment, Olivier Chandon of the champagne Chandons', before he flipped his race car into a canal in Florida and went terminal bye-bye, Andy Rooney of *60 Minutes* and I co-wrote a script for a TV skydiving film that I co-directed.

When I worked in films I met and spent some time with Maxamillian Schell, Robert Redford, Joan Crawford, Martin Sheen, and a lot of others.

My partner, Tammy, was named Woman of the Year by the National MS Society for leading one of the first all-woman's skydiving teams and starring in a skydiving public service commercial. At the awards banquet we dined with Frank and Kathy Lee Gifford, Florence Griffith-Joyner, the President of Paramount, Ed McMahon and The Prez at the time, Bush #1, presented the award by video link.

Doing demonstration jumps for various events I've had photo-ops with Yogi Berra, Governors' Christy Whitman, Brendan Byrne, and many lesser politicos. This wasn't new stuff to me and I'm usually pretty cool with royalty but John-John was going to be a serious challenge. I went to lunch.

The airport restaurant was a couple of hundred yards from our hangar and when I entered the place was crowded with first jumpers, staff, and pilots, wolfing down greasy cheeseburgers, soggy French fries, and blabbing about their various aviation adventures.

I found a seat at the counter and ordered something quick to go. While I waited I spotted John and his buddies at a corner table and no one seemed to be paying much attention. So far, so good. I was hoping that we could get the day over and John and the guys back in their BMW heading to the Big Apple before the *National Enquirer* arrived.

Because Skydive East was responsible for most of the pesos' that came through the restaurant's coffers I had my order in a couple of minutes and Marie leaned over the counter as she handed it to me and I knew she was in on the big news.

"I gotta' get a picture with him," she kind of asked me.

Marie was in her sixties', several hundred pounds and dentally challenged. Her ratty apron held remnants of whatever was on the menu that day and the armpits of her 1940's style dress were soggy from the sweltering kitchen. No Way.

Actually I told her that if she would keep her mouth shut about who he was I'd see what I could do after John had made his jump. I was lying.

I stopped by the office on my way to the training area and put an embargo on any information about John. I knew that the news was bound to gravitate outside the airport boundaries before the end of the day and was determined to keep herds of groupies, or worse yet, reporters, from showing up. The girls who answered the phones were to disavow any knowledge of our superstar student.

As we waited for the last stragglers to show up for the outdoor training I struck up a conversation with John and his friends, George, Rob, and Ed and found that they all worked in the New York DA's office. John had just taken the bar exam for the second time and was sweating out the results, probably the result of a lot of family and media pressure. They were a nice group of guys and I felt that they would do well on their jump.

When the last few students wandered in, still finishing their burgers and fries, I did a head count and started aircraft exit practice, moved on to emergency procedures and parachute landing falls.

By three o'clock the class was ready to jump and I assigned them to their flights in groups of four and sent them over to the flight line where our two Cessnas' and the ground crew were standing by to get the students into their parachutes. Broken clouds were starting to filter in from the south but they were still above jump altitude, three thousand feet, so it looked like we would get most of the class out.

I picked up my parachute at the hangar and gave a copy of the manifest sheets to Harry, the ground instructor, so he'd know the name of the person he was talking to on the ground-to-air radio. John would be the last person to jump on the second flight. I reminded Harry that if John didn't land on the drop zone Harry would be living in the woods and eating out of dumpsters for the rest of his life.

I slipped into my rig and gave the first flight an equipment check and last minute briefing as the pilot cranked up the 182. We climbed aboard and were soon airborne and headed south to the drop zone.

We were at twenty five hundred feet by the time we were over the landing area and dropped a wind streamer, determined the exit point and circled for the first jump run. As I got the first student into the door we flew through a small cloud but I could see more moving toward us as #1 climbed onto the step and launched into a fairly good semblance of an arch and spread.

After pulling in the static line deployment bag I scribbled his grade on the manifest sheet and moved #2 into the door and in eight minutes we were empty and diving back to the airport to pick up the second flight. Though I had my emotions under control during the day I couldn't avoid thinking of all of the things that could go wrong and the possible repercussions. I had maximum confidence in our student parachutes and radio systems but parachute malfunctions do occur and radios' do occasionally fail. It's Murphy's Law that they always do at the worst time. I consoled myself when I realized that I'd gone through the same thought process when I tossed my son out a few years before on his sixteenth birthday.

We landed and taxied to pick up flight two, waiting in their forty pounds of parachutes, boot, and helmets. My good friend and jumpmaster, Bob, was with them, his Nikon hanging around his neck.

Though I had spent the day making sure that John wasn't bugged by the paparazzi I sure as hell wasn't going to let this occasion pass without a shot for my photo wall. John didn't object and I promised that no one else would get their hands on them so Bob snapped away as I checked their equipment and herded them into the plane, closed the jump door, and we were airborne.

Over the drop zone the clouds were getting thicker but there were still enough holes to get the first three guys out safely. I moved John into the door and had him put his feet on the step as the pilot rolled onto jump run. As I stuck my head out and looked down there was just a blanket of white blocking out the ground below. We were going to have to go around.

It's really hard to communicate verbally with any one in a jump plane. The door's open, the roar of the engine is deafening and the helmet covering the student's ears make it worse. I pointed at the clouds and motioned for him to pull his legs back in as we went around for another pass. This is tough for a first time jumper, you've got your nerve up for the jump, the adrenaline is pumping, and then something goes wrong. I banged him on the helmet and gave him a thumbs' up and when he smiled and returned the gesture I knew he was okay with it.

The next pass was dicey but we had a hole just as we hit the exit point and he climbed out onto the step and when I gave him the command to go he launched into a perfect arch and spread, smiling back at me in the door until his 'chute opened. Whew!

We circled over the drop zone as John steered in and landed right on the target and was up on his feet, all of his extremities apparently intact. I radioed Harry and gave him a raise.

After the third flight the ceiling had dropped to two grand and was now solid so we packed it in for the day and gave rain checks to the remaining students and I de-briefed the three flights that had jumped, handed out their first jump certificates, and gave them our sales pitch for t-shirts and second jump tickets before they went on their way.

Monday morning our phone lines were jammed with media inquires but we gave them our "sorry we can't give out information on our clients" routine. *People* magazine was particularly insistent, offering serious money for the story and any photos that we had, as did several tabloids. We didn't give them anything.

Gossip columnist, Liz Smith, had a snarky item in her column wondering why John was skydiving at Skydive East rather than studying for the bar exam but that was just good publicity for us.

And then there was Marie. I don't know when or how she did it but she has an eleven by fourteen of her kissing John. It's her most prized possession.

Chapter 25

Hubble

On December 2nd, 1993, I stood shivering with my partner, Tammy, and our close friends, Bob and Emma, in the predawn darkness in the parking lot of a bar in Titusville, Florida. It was 4 AM and we were a little hung over and sleep deprived as we stared across the Indian River where the space shuttle Endeavour stood bathed in light as the crew counted down for a launch that would take them on an eleven day mission to repair the Hubble telescope, orbiting 329 miles above earth.

None of us had seen a launch before and probably wouldn't have driven a thousand miles from New Jersey to see this one but I had a personal connection to two of the astronauts, Jeff Hoffman and Story Musgrave, and had to be here.

Soon after we built the Lakewood Parachute Center, Story showed up in a first jump class that I was teaching. He didn't stand out in the twenty or so people in the class; less than average height, prematurely bald though only in his late twenties, and didn't look like the macho type. He made his first static line jump that day and returned for subsequent jumps as he tried to work his way onto freefall, which required five stable exits and simulated ripcord pulls.

It didn't go well at first. Story would be cleared for freefall, have a couple of unstable exits, and be returned to static line. This process continued for a long time during which the Navy transferred me to Rhode Island and I started working at Orange on weekends and had lost track of his progress until a few years later when someone mentioned that Story, after zigging and zagging back and forth from freefall to static line had finally completed the student program and was an experienced jumper.

I mentioned Jeff Hoffman and his brother Bob in the high jump story. Sons of a prominent orthopedic surgeon they were in their late teens and students at the University of Massachusetts at that time.

Unlike Story, Bob and Jeff, already experienced skiers and mountain climbers, had an easy time progressing quickly through the student program and becoming proficient skydivers.

After I left Orange, Bob and I maintained a close friendship but I hadn't heard from Jeff for a while until I received a letter in August of 1993. It was from Jeff and the return address was NASA.

Jeff and Story were going to be mission specialists on the upcoming flight of the Endeavor to repair the Hubble Telescope and they were inviting me to the launch.

I already knew that they were astronauts. They had both flown on several shuttle missions and Bob kept me posted on Jeff's flights but I'd never seen a launch and wasn't going to miss this one. I rsvp'd and a couple of weeks later received four passes for the blast off and an invitation to the pre-launch luncheon for friends and families of the crew.

The Endeavour was to lift off at 5:30 AM on the first of December. Our posse of four left New Jersey two days after Thanksgiving and were on I-95 headed for the Sunshine State.

We pulled into South of The Border, our halfway point, just before dark, our throats parched from singing ninety-nine bottles of beer on the wall.

If you live on the east coast you've been to, or at least passed, South of the Border. There are billboards every couple of miles for two hours north and south featuring Pedro in his sombrero offering corny jokes about the place. Straddling the state line of North and South Carolina it's a sprawling complex of Mexican themed motel rooms, restaurants, and cheap souvenir shops. Another attraction is a vast fireworks warehouse selling everything from sparklers to small nuclear weapons. There's also a two hundred foot tower in the middle of the complex topped by a giant sombrero that's visible from miles away.

We checked in, got our bar set up, and caught the news. The shuttle flight was featured, as it had been for the last week. The astronauts were scheduled to make five space walks to repair the telescope which was impaired by an improperly ground mirror that was producing blurry images. They were going to fit it with what was described as a giant contact lens to compensate for the defect. Conditions looked favorable for the launch on the 1st.

We made it to our lodging in Titusville late the next afternoon and hooked up with Jeff's brother Bob. Over drinks and dinner he told us about the mission. He also warned us that the launch would blow our minds.

With two days to kill before the blast off we spent the next day doing the tourist routine at the Cape. I was stationed in Sanford, about thirty miles from the Space Center when I was in the Navy and often fished in the Indian River that borders the complex but had never seen the displays and artifacts of previous space flights which included rockets and capsules that spanned the history of U.S space flight. Way cool!

The following day we met the families of the crew at the traditional pre-launch party at the HoJo hotel in Coco Beach (the astronauts were in quarantine) and bedded down early in preparation for the following morning's five AM launch.

Our invitations included passes to the private viewing area for friends and families on the NASA causeway, about a half mile from the launch pad where the countdown was underway.

We staked out a spot and Bob and I set up our cameras. Loudspeakers were broadcasting the chatter between the crew and mission control as well as the countdown to launch as tension and excitement built up in our fellow spectators and us.

At T minus :30 the countdown went on hold, started again, and went on hold again as a NASA jet appeared and did several touch and go's on the shuttle landing strip adjacent to the launch pad. Though the pre-dawn sky was full of stars we eventually learned from the mission control transmissions to the shuttle that the cross wind on the runway, where the shuttle would have to make an emergency landing if something went wrong in the first few minutes after launch, was higher than safe limits and as dawn broke over the Atlantic, the launch window had passed and the flight was scrubbed and re-scheduled for the next morning.

We were seriously bummed out as we packed up our camera gear and thermos jugs and headed back to town. Of course we knew that launches are often cancelled but because it was a clear night never considered that a stupid fifteen mile an hour crosswind would ruin our day. I tried not to think about all of the shuttle flights that had been delayed for months for various reasons and wondered how the crew strapped into their seats for the last five hours felt.

The chilly Florida morning turned hot and sunny. After breakfast we laid around the motel pool most of the afternoon, frying our lily-white skin and drinking Bloody Marys' as we listened to weather reports. The chances for the next day were 50-50.

I called Bob and asked him to join us for dinner. He was free and suggested a place on the Indian River in Titusville. The restaurant was a hang-out for workers from the space center, the walls covered with pictures of rockets and astronauts. Our table was next to a picture window with a great view of the Cape and Endeavour perched on the launch pad.

As we waited for Bob the owner asked us if we were in town for the launch and we related our morning disappointment. He suggested that we avoid the traffic and security and watch the launch from the restaurant parking lot which was just a mile from our motel and actually closer to the launch than our spots in the VIP area at the Cape. We took him up on it.

Bob showed up and told us that the lift-off was now scheduled for 4 AM and the forecast was a little iffy but they were going to try. He'd spoken to Jeff and the crew was upbeat and ready to fly.

After a few hours of fitful sleep we joined a dozen others in the restaurant parking lot an hour before the scheduled lift-off. We missed having the loudspeaker transmissions that followed the countdown but the view of the shuttle across the river was perfect and a nearby portable radio was keeping us posted.

At 4:27 AM the main engines ignited and the Endeavour seemed engulfed in a ball of fire from an explosion that lit up everything for miles, the launch pad, river, and the parking lot where we stood. The ground shuddered as the shuttle inched its way into the air, spewing orange and red fire as it started to accelerate toward orbital speed.

It was probably the most impressive thing that I'd ever seen and I couldn't quite wrap my mind around the fact that Jeff and Story were inside that thing. That's some balls! We've all seen launches on the tube but to see a night launch up close and personal should be on everyone's bucket list.

When the shuttle was well out of sight we drove back to the motel, stunned by our near religious experience, and watched it reach orbit on TV as we packed up and headed back north.

For the next ten days I was glued to the set as Jeff and Story alternated with the second team of space-walkers, Tom Akers and Kathryn Thornton, as they accomplished the greatest mission since the moon landing, repairing and performing maintenance on the Hubble which has allowed a quantum leap in our ability to peer deep into space and probe the farthest reaches of the universe.

This book has been about people; clowns and crooks, heroes and hookers, dopers and drunks, celebrities and ne'er do wells, saints and sinners (lots of sinners). Most of them were skydivers, a few pilots, and some friends and people I've run into during my life. Jeff and Story are two of them and I like to think that teaching them to jump out of airplanes planted a small seed that helped them on their path into space.

The End